Co-operative Banks in India and Select Countries

Co-operative Banks in India and Select Countries

By

S. Nakkiran
Professor, Department of Co-operatives,
Ambo University, Ethiopia

R. Karunakaran
Assistant Professor, Department of Co-operatives,
Hawassa University, Ethiopia

V. Natarajan
Assistant Professor, Department of Co-operatives,
Ambo University, Ethiopia

New Century Publications
New Delhi, India

NEW CENTURY PUBLICATIONS
4800/24, Bharat Ram Road,
Ansari Road, Daryaganj,
New Delhi - 110 002 (India)

Tel.: 011-2324 7798, 4358 7398, 6539 6605
Fax: 011-4101 7798
E-mail: indiatax@vsnl.com • info@newcenturypublications.com
www.newcenturypublications.com

Editorial office:
LG-7, Aakarshan Bhawan,
4754-57/23, Ansari Road, Daryaganj,
New Delhi - 110 002

Tel.: 011-4356 0919

First Published: **2014**

ISBN: **978-81-7708-375-0**

Published by New Century Publications and printed at Salasar Imaging Systems, New Delhi.

Designs: Patch Creative Unit, New Delhi.

PRINTED IN INDIA

About the Book

In a market-oriented economy, the terms of contract are frequently weighted in favour of persons of large means. Those who have the command of scarce resources are left free to drive a bargain with those who need such resources but are ill-equipped to compete for their possession. Co-operatives are institutional agencies for achieving social cohesion. In a country whose economic structure has its roots in the villages, co-operation is something more than a series of activities organised on co-operative lines. Basically, its purpose is to evolve a system of co-operative community organisation which touches upon all aspects of life.

Co-operatives in India started as a means of ensuring, for the poorly equipped citizens, advantages which better placed persons were able to command by their own individual resources. The principle of mutual aid, which is the basis of co-operative organisation, and the practice of thrift and self-help which sustains it, generate a sturdy feeling of self-reliance which is of basic importance in a democratic way of life. By pooling their experience and knowledge and by helping one another, members of co-operative societies cannot only find the solutions of individual problems but also become better citizens.

The present work explains and examines the functioning of co-operative banks in India and select other countries— including Grameen Bank of Bangladesh—to understand their role in the globalized world.

About the Authors

Professor S. Nakkiran (1945) is presently Professor, Department of Co-operatives, Ambo University, Ethiopia. He has written 21 books in the areas of research methodology, management and co-operation. He has undertaken several independent research projects. Widely travelled, he is an authority on co-operative studies.

Dr. R. Karunakaran (1966) is currently Assistant Professor, Department of Co-operatives, Hawassa University, Ethiopia. He has published more than 30 research papers in reputed Indian and international journals.

Dr. V. Natarajan (1958) is presently Assistant Professor, Department of Co-operatives, Ambo University, Ethiopia. He has contributed research papers to several international journals.

Contents

Preface

Co-operatives are institutional agencies for achieving social cohesion. In a country whose economic structure has its roots in the village, co-operation is something more than a series of activities organised on co-operative lines. Basically, its purpose is to evolve a system of co-operative community organisation which touches upon all aspects of life. Within the village community there are sections of the population who need special assistance. Co-operation should therefore mean an obligation towards all families in the village community and the development of land and other resources and of social services in the common interest of the village as a whole. This is the underlying approach in setting co-operative village management as the main direction of reorganisation in the rural economy.

In India, as in many other countries, co-operation started as a means of ensuring for the poorly equipped citizens advantages which better placed persons were able to command by their own individual resources. The principle of mutual aid, which is the basis of co-operative organisation, and the practice of thrift and self-help which sustain it, generate a sturdy feeling of self-reliance which is of basic importance in a democratic way of life. By pooling their experience and knowledge and by helping one another, members of co-operative societies cannot only find the solutions of individual problems but also become better citizens.

In an unregulated economy, the terms of contract are frequently weighted in favour of persons of large means. Those who have the command of scarce resources are left free to drive a bargain with those who need such resources but are ill-equipped to compete for their possession. In a relatively stagnant agricultural economy of small holders, undergoing a transition from barter to money economy and from local to national and international exchange, the possession of capital naturally confers a strategic advantage.

An increasing measure of responsibility for organising and financing rural economic development is being shouldered by co-operatives. Both the natural evolution of co-operative activity, and the impetus of the special need created in several parts of the country by agrarian legislation regulating the business of moneylenders, scaling down of debts, restricting rents and abolishing landlordism are responsible for the striking increase in the operations of co-operative credit societies.

Having begun primarily in the field of credit as a defensive mechanism against the usurious money lenders, co-operatives have come to embrace a large gamut of activities to serve the interests of the producers and consumers. Credit, however, still continues to be the predominant activity.

Co-operatives are expected to play a major role in the distribution of inputs and services to the farmers on the one hand and in assisting marketing and processing of agricultural produce on the other.

Even more striking than the expansion in numbers and size, is the growing diversity of functions assumed by co-operative societies. Besides agricultural societies of all types, viz. credit, processing, marketing, farming, irrigation, consolidation etc., there are industrial co-operatives, labour societies, consumers' co-operatives in rural as well as in urban areas, housing societies; processing factories; and urban banks.

When co-operation was first introduced under the Co-operative Credit Societies Act, 1904, it was confined to the organisation of the co-operative credit societies in urban and rural areas with a view to relieving indebtedness and promoting thrift. The Co-operative Societies Act, 1912, permitted the registration of co-operative societies for promoting non-credit activities as well as federations of primary societies into organisations at higher levels. Both in the field of credit and of non-credit activities, the co-operative structure consists of primary societies at the base in villages or towns, central organisations at the district level and apex organisations at the State level.

Co-operatives in India came into being as a result of the Government taking cognizance of the agricultural conditions that prevailed during the latter part of the 19th century and the absence of institutional arrangements for finance to agriculturists, which had resulted in mounting distress and discontent. Small, local, locally worked institutions, co-operative in form, which would satisfy the postulates of proximity, security and facility for providing credit, were seen as the answer to this situation. However, subsequent events during both pre- and post-Independence period have led to a vast growth of co-operatives covering various sectors of the Indian economy.

Though India can claim to have the world's largest and most diverse co-operative movement, barring some exceptions co-operatives in India, in general, are fraught with a number of problems and challenges. Apart from certain inherent weaknesses, they are constrained by the overwhelming role of the government as well as prescriptive and restrictive legislation and have been unable to retain an autonomous and democratic character.

Co-operatives are often criticised for being dominated by vested interests. The solutions sought so far have been in the nature of limiting the number of terms of office etc. While these measures are useful as far as they go, they still do not impinge on the basic question of commitment of an office bearer to the objectives of the society. An office bearer of a marketing society, who does not market his own produce through his marketing co-operative, is hardly likely to have any stake in the performance of that society.

The success of co-operatives ultimately depends upon their ability to perform their functions—whether they relate to production, finance, marketing, distribution or construction—efficiently and to the satisfaction of the members and the community. The loyalties of the members can be retained not on the basis of monopoly, agreements or under duress but on the strength of the goodwill secured by rendering service.

The global economy, and in particular the Indian economy, is passing through transformation. The positive dimension of globalization includes liberal economic policies, reduction of state intervention, and easy access to monetary capital and consequently new opportunities for economic participation. This is already evidenced in India in the form of increased economic growth and state withdrawal from many economic and social domains. On the other hand, there is apparently a misplaced perception developing in India that co-operatives may not be able to deliver in the context of the globalized market conditions and the changes that are taking place as a result.

Under the circumstances, there is a need for resurgence of co-operatives as important players. Co-operatives have tremendous opportunities because: (a) they have a special identity, (b) they have both social and economic objectives, (c) they are value- and community-based, (d) they are people-oriented, and (e) they have a network of linkages through the co-operative movement.

Ethiopia

S. Nakkiran
R. Karunakaran
V. Natarajan

1

Financial Inclusion of the Poor: Policies and Measures

Rapid economic growth in India in recent years has brought in its wake a number of concerns, which relate to expanding this growth across regions, sectors, and people. The major objective of India's Twelfth Five Year Plan (2012-17) is to ensure inclusive growth by removing the constraints of poor infrastructure, improving economic efficiency and spreading the benefits of growth over a vast population, which has remained outside the purview of development efforts. The financial sector in the country has also experienced revolutionary changes, but it has by passed a large segment of population.

The objective of financial inclusion is to extend financial services to the large hitherto unserved population of the country to unlock its growth potential. In addition, it strives towards a more inclusive growth by making financing available to the poor in particular. Government of India has been actively pursuing the agenda of financial inclusion, with key interventions in four groups, viz. expanding banking infrastructure, offering appropriate financial products, making extensive and intensive use of technology and through advocacy and stakeholder participation.

1.1 Social Control over Commercial Banks

Financial inclusion, in the sense of extending banking products at an affordable cost to the vast sections of disadvantaged and low income groups, is not new to India. With a view to better aligning the banking system to the needs of planning and economic policy, the policy of social control over the banking sector began in 1967. The year 1969 was a landmark in the history of commercial banking in India. In July of that year, the government nationalised 14 major commercial banks of the country. In April 1980, government nationalised 6 more commercial banks. Leading commercial banks of the country were nationalised with the following objectives in view.

1. To break the ownership and control of banks by a few business families.
2. To prevent concentration of wealth and economic power.
3. To mobilise savings of the masses from every nook and corner of the country.
4. To pay greater attention to the credit needs of the priority sectors like agriculture and small industries.

With the nationalisation of these banks, the major segment of the banking sector came under the control of the Government. Massive expansion of the branch network that followed the nationalisation of banks resulted in large deposit mobilisation by banks, which helped in stepping up the overall savings rate of the economy. However, during this period, a major portion of resources of the banks were pre-empted at below market rates by way of directed credit and directed investments. Profitability of the banking sector was, therefore, affected. Banks were also saddled with large non-performing assets. Their capital base also became weak.

The nationalisation of banks was an attempt to use the scarce resources of the banking system for the purpose of planned development. The task of maintaining a large number of small accounts was not profitable for the banks as a result of which they had limited lending in the rural sector. The problem of lopsided distribution of banks and the lack of explicit articulation of the need to channel credit to certain priority sectors was sought to be achieved through nationalisation policy. The Lead Bank Scheme provided the blueprint of further bank branch expansion.

The biggest achievement of nationalisation was the reallocation of sectoral credit in favour of agriculture, small industries and exports which formed the core of the priority sector. Within agriculture, credit for the procurement of food grains (food credit) was a major item. Other agricultural activities preferred for credit included poultry farming, dairy, and piggeries. Certain other sectors of the economy which also received attention for credit allocation were: professionals and self-employed persons, artisans and weaker sections of society. Conversely, there was a sharp fall in bank credit to large-scale industries. However, the share of small-scale industry registered an upward trend.

Nationalisation of commercial banks was a mixed blessing. After nationalisation there was a shift of emphasis from industry to agriculture. The country witnessed rapid expansion in bank branches, even in rural areas. Branch expansion programme led to mobilisation of savings from all parts of the country. Nationalised banks were able to pay attention to the credit needs of weaker sections, artisans and self-employed. However, bank nationalisation created its own problems like excessive bureaucratisation, red-tapism and disruptive tactics of trade unions of bank employees. There are concerns that banks have still not been able to reach a vast segment of the population and provide them with basic banking services.

1.2 Financial Exclusion and Financial Inclusion Defined

In most developing countries, a large segment of society, particularly low-income people, has very little access to financial services, both formal and semi-formal. As a consequence, many of them have to necessarily depend either on their own or high cost informal sources of finance such as moneylenders. This is particularly true for the sporadic financing requirements of low income households for non-productive consumption purposes and other emergency requirements such as medical expenditure. Benefits of growth, therefore, tend to concentrate in the hands of those already served by the formal financial system.

1.2.1 Financial Exclusion: Despite the rapid spread of banking over the years, a significant segment of the population, predominantly in the rural areas, is excluded from the formal financial system. It is well-known that poor people, potential entrepreneurs, small enterprises and others are excluded from the financial sector, which leads to their marginalisation and denial of opportunity for them to grow and prosper. Therefore, access to a greater proportion of the population to the organised financial system should be high on the agenda of the Government of India. The key issue, however, is how to mainstream the institutional sources so as to achieve wider coverage in terms of extending credit. There are also a large number of households with low income and small savings, which need to be mobilised.

Apart from the rural areas, there is significant degree of financial exclusion in urban areas as well. The cost of financial exclusion is recognised to be enormous for the society as well as for individuals, particularly in terms of inability to realise full potential due to financial constraints.

The recent developments in banking technology have transformed banking from the traditional brick-and-mortar infrastructure like staffed branches to a system supplemented by other channels like automated teller machines (ATM), credit/debit cards, internet banking, online money transfers etc. However, the access to such technology is restricted only to certain segments of the society. Indeed, some trends, such as increasingly sophisticated customer segmentation technology—allowing, for example, more accurate targeting of sections of the market—have led to restricted access to financial services for some groups. There is a growing divide, with an increased range of personal finance options for a segment of high and upper middle income population and a significantly large section of the population who lack access to even the most basic banking services. This is termed *financial exclusion*. These people, particularly, those living on low incomes, cannot access mainstream financial products such as bank accounts, credit, remittances and payment services, financial advisory services, insurance facilities etc.

Merely having a bank account may not be a good indicator of financial inclusion. The ideal definition should look at people who want to access financial services but are denied the same. If genuine claimants for credit and financial services are denied the same, then that is a case of exclusion. As this aspect would raise the issue of credit worthiness or bankability, it is also necessary to dwell upon what could be done to make the claimants of institutional credit bankable or creditworthy. This would require re-engineering of existing financial products or delivery systems and making them more in tune with the expectations and absorptive capacity of the intended clientele.

1.2.2 Financial Inclusion: According to the Committee on Financial Inclusion (Chairman: C. Rangarajan), 2008, "Financial inclusion may be defined as the process of ensuring access to financial services and timely and adequate credit where needed by vulnerable groups such as weaker sections and low income groups at an affordable cost."

The essence of financial inclusion is in trying to ensure that a range of appropriate financial services is available to every individual and enabling them to understand and access those services. Apart from the regular form of financial intermediation, it may include a basic no-frills banking account for making and receiving payments, a savings product suited to the pattern of cash flows of a poor household, money transfer facilities, small loans and overdrafts for productive, personal and other purposes, insurance (life and non-life) etc. While financial inclusion, in the narrow sense, may be achieved to some extent by offering any one of these services, the objective of *comprehensive financial inclusion* would be to provide a holistic set of services encompassing all of the above.

1.3 Advantages of Financial Inclusion

Access to safe, easy and affordable credit and other financial services by the poor and vulnerable groups, disadvantaged areas and lagging sectors is recognised as a precondition for accelerating growth and reducing income disparities and poverty. A developing country can benefit from financial inclusion in the following ways:

1. Access to a well-functioning financial system—by creating equal opportunities—enables economically and socially excluded people to integrate effectively into the economy and contribute to development and protect themselves against economic shocks.
2. Financial inclusion enables to finance activities or firms or individuals that are at the margin, thereby promoting their growth-inducing productive activities.
3. Availability of external finance to potential entrepreneurs and small firms enables new entrants, leading to increased competition to incumbents. This, in turn, encourages entrepreneurship and productivity.
4. Inclusive finance—including safe savings, appropriately designed loans for poor and low-income households and for micro, small and medium-sized enterprises, and appropriate insurance and payments services—can help people to enhance incomes, acquire capital, manage risk, and come out of poverty.
5. It has been well-recognised that access to financial services facilitates making and receiving financial payments and reduces transaction costs.
6. Access to financial services contributes to higher production and social protection, as the financial sector—through stored savings, credit and insurance—serves as a measure of crisis mitigation.

1.4 Strategy for Building an Inclusive Financial Sector

Bringing the larger population within the structured and organised financial system has to be an important item on the development agenda of a government. While several central banks focus solely on inflation, many in developed and emerging economies alike, including India, also focus on growth. The RBI has, therefore, introduced various new measures to encourage the expansion of financial coverage in the country. Financial inclusion is considered essential for fostering economic growth in a more inclusive fashion.

In a fast growing economy, an important issue is how to sustain and diversify growth so that the risk to growth process is diversified across sectors. It is in this context that the search for potential sources of incremental growth, i.e. sectors that have difficulty in accessing financial services, assumes importance. Therefore, including such segments or sectors would, on the one hand, unleash their productive capacities, and on the other, would augment domestic demand on a sustainable basis driven by income and consumption growth from such sectors. This would also have strong inter-sectoral linkages.

Overall strategy for building an inclusive financial sector may be based on:

1. Effecting improvements within the existing formal credit delivery mechanism,
2. Measures for improving credit absorption capacity especially amongst marginal and sub marginal farmers and poor non-cultivator households,
3. Evolving new models for effective outreach, and
4. Leveraging on technology based solutions.

1.5 Recent Measures for Financial Inclusion

Given the socio-demographic complexities in India, the policy endeavour of the RBI has been to adopt a multi-institutional and multi-instrument approach to comprehensively address the issue of financial inclusion in all its dimensions, going beyond mere availability of credit to the masses. Thc term *financial inclusion* needs to be understood in a broader perspective to mean the provision of the full range of affordable financial services, viz. access to payments and remittance facilities, savings, loans and insurance services by the formal financial system to those who tend to be excluded from these services. The RBI, while recognising the concerns in regard to the banking practices that tend to exclude rather than attract vast sections of population, has been urging the banks to review their existing practices to align them with the objective of achieving greater financial inclusion. The RBI too has taken a number of measures with the objective of attracting the financially excluded population into the formalised financial system. Some of the measures taken in this direction are as follows.

1.5.1 No Frills Account: With a view to achieving greater financial inclusion, banks were advised in November 2005 to make available a basic banking *no frills account* either with 'nil' or very low minimum balances as well as charges that would make such accounts accessible to vast sections of population. All the public and the private sector banks as well as the foreign banks, except those not having significant retail presence, are reported to have introduced the basic banking 'no-frills' account.

1.5.2 General Credit Card (GCC): With the objective of providing hassle-free credit to the banks' constituents in rural and semi urban areas, the banks were advised in December 2005, to consider introduction of a *General Credit Card* (GCC) to such constituents. The card was to have a credit limit of up to ₹ 25,000, based on the assessment of income and cash flows of the household without insistence on security or purpose or end-use of credit. The credit facility was to be in the nature of revolving credit entitling the holder to withdraw up to the limit sanctioned. The banks are required to charge appropriate and reasonable Interest rate on the facility.

1.5.3 Business Facilitator and Business Correspondent (BC) Models: In January 2006, banks were permitted to utilise the services of non-governmental organisations (NGOs/SHGs), micro-finance institutions and other civil society organisations as intermediaries in providing financial and banking services through the use of *business facilitator* and *business correspondent (BC)* models. The BC model allows banks to do *cash in-cash out* transactions at the location of the BC and allows branchless banking.

1.5.4 Passbook Facility: The matter of issuing passbooks to the small depositors has been a nagging issue for sometime past. Pass books provide the account holders a ready reckoner of the transactions in their accounts and is a convenient reference document—which cannot be substituted by periodical bank account statements, particularly by the small account holders. Since non-issuance of the pass books to the small customers could indirectly lead to their financial exclusion, the RBI had advised the banks in October 2006 to invariably offer the pass book facility to all its savings bank account holders (individuals) and not to levy any charge on the customers thereof.

1.5.5 Simplified KYC Procedure: With a view to facilitating the opening of bank accounts by the common man through a simplified KYC procedure, in the Mid-Term Review of the Annual Policy of the RBI for the year 2006-07, it was announced that the "banks could open accounts of low balance/turnover (where the balance does not exceed ₹ 50,000 in all the accounts taken together and the total credit in all the accounts taken together is not expected to exceed rupees two lakh in a year) only with self certification of address by the customers and his photograph". However, this policy announcement is yet to be operationalised as the matter is under consideration of the Government in the light of the provisions of the Rules framed under Prevention of Money Laundering Act.

1.5.6 Credit Counselling and Financial Education: Promoting *credit counselling and financial education* of the clientele of the banks is also an area that deserves due attention of the banking community. Towards this objective, the banks were also advised by the RBI to make available all printed material used by retail customers in the concerned regional language. As far as RBI itself is concerned, it has launched on June 18, 2007, a multilingual website in 13 Indian languages on all matters concerning banking and the common person so that the language does not become a barrier to acquiring financial education by the public at large.

1.6 Committee on Financial Inclusion

Committee on Financial Inclusion (Chairman: C. Rangarajan) was constituted by the Government of India on June 26, 2006 to prepare a strategy of financial inclusion. The Committee submitted its Final Report on January 4, 2008. The Report viewed financial inclusion as a comprehensive and holistic process of ensuring access to financial services and timely and adequate credit, particularly to vulnerable groups such as weaker sections and low income groups at an affordable cost. Financial inclusion, therefore, according to the Committee, should include access to mainstream financial products such as bank accounts, credit, remittances and payment services, financial advisory services and insurance facilities.

The Report observed that in India 51.4 percent of farmer households are financially excluded from both formal/informal sources and 73 percent of farmer households do not access formal sources of credit. Exclusion is most acute in Central, Eastern and North-Eastern regions with 64 percent of all financially excluded farmer households. According to the Report, the overall strategy for building an inclusive financial sector should be based on the following policy measures:

1. Effecting improvements within the existing formal credit delivery mechanism.
2. Suggesting measures for improving credit absorption capacity especially amongst marginal and sub-marginal farmers and poor non-cultivator households.
3. Evolving new models for effective outreach.
4. Leveraging on technology based solutions.

Keeping in view the enormity of the task involved, the Committee recommended the setting up of a mission mode National Rural Financial Inclusion Plan (NRFIP) with a target of providing access to comprehensive financial services to at least 50 percent (55.77 million) of the excluded rural households by 2012 and the remaining by 2015. This would require semi-urban and rural branches of commercial banks and RRBs to cover a minimum of 250 new cultivator and non-cultivator households per branch per annum. The Committee also recommended that the Government should constitute a National Mission on Financial Inclusion (NaMFI) comprising representatives of all stakeholders for suggesting the overall policy changes required, and supporting stakeholders in the domain of public, private and NGO sectors in undertaking promotional initiatives.

The major recommendations relating to commercial banks included: (a) target for providing access to credit to at least 250 excluded rural households per annum in each rural/semi-urban branches, (b) targeted branch expansion in identified districts in the next three years, (c) provision of customised savings, credit and insurance products, (d) incentivising human resources for providing inclusive financial services, and (e) simplification of procedures for agricultural loans.

The major recommendations relating to regional rural banks (RRBs) included: (a) extending their services to unbanked areas and increasing their credit-deposit ratios, (b) no further merger of RRBs, (c) widening of network and expanding coverage in a time-bound manner, and (d) separate credit plans for excluded regions and strengthening of their boards.

In the case of co-operative banks, the major recommendations were: (a) early implementation of Vaidyanathan Committee Revival Package, (b) use of primary agricultural credit societies (PACS) and other primary co-operatives as business correspondents, and (c) co-operatives to adopt group approach for financing excluded groups.

Other important recommendations of the Committee included: (a) encouraging self-help groups (SHGs) in excluded regions, (b) legal status for SHGs and (c) measures for urban micro-finance and separate category of micro finance institutions (MFIs).

The Committee recommended setting up of two funds: Financial Inclusion Fund (FIF) and Financial Inclusion Technology Fund (FITF). Each of the Funds shall consist of an overall corpus of ₹ 500 crore, with initial funding to be contributed by the Government of India, Reserve Bank of India (RBI) and NABARD in the ratio of 40:40:20.

The two funds have been established with NABARD which is the coordinating agency for financial inclusion initiatives with its Financial Inclusion Department (FID) as the nodal department. The core activities of the FID are to carry forward the agenda of financial inclusion of the excluded population at the national level as per the framework described by the Committee on Financial Inclusion in general and operationalising the Financial Inclusion Fund (FIF) and Financial Inclusion Technology Fund (FITF), in particular. The implementation is under the guidance of the two Advisory Boards set up for FIF and FITF respectively.

1.6.1 Financial Inclusion Fund (FIF): The objective of FIF is to support "developmental and promotional activities" with a view to securing greater financial inclusion, particularly among weaker sections, low income groups and in backward regions/hitherto unbanked areas.

A. Eligible Activities/Purposes: These are as under:

1. Funding support for capacity building inputs to business facilitators and business correspondents.
2. Providing promotional support to institutions, such as resource centres, farmers' service centres and rural development and self-employment training institutes to enable them to provide improved technical and financial services (including counseling) aimed at increasing technology adoption, effective management of assets, nurturing entrepreneurial capacity and increasing financial education and literacy.
3. Providing funding support for promotion, nurturing and credit linking of self-help groups (SHGs).
4. Capacity building of personnel of NABARD, banks, post

offices, State Government Departments, micro finance institutions, NGOs, local level associations, members of SHGs/joint liability groups etc.

5. Defraying expenses of approved institutions for undertaking interventions for financial inclusion in Central, Eastern and North-east Regions; Jammu and Kashmir, Himachal Pradesh and Uttarakhand.
6. Funding support for setting up of rural credit bureaus and credit rating of rural customers.
7. Supporting initiatives of local level associations.
8. Supporting pilot projects for development of innovative products, processes and prototypes for financial inclusion.
9. Any other developmental and promotional interventions recommended by the advisory board for the FIF.

B. Eligible Institutions: These are as under:

1. Financial Institutions, viz. NABARD, commercial banks, regional rural banks (RRBs) and cooperative banks;
2. NGOs, MFIs, SHGs, farmers' clubs, local level associations etc.
3. Training and research organisations, academic institutions, universities.
4. Service providers like insurance companies (providing micro insurance services), post offices, railways etc.
5. Any other organisation whose objectives are in conformity with the overall objectives of the FIF and are approved by the Advisory Board from time to time.

1.6.2 Financial Inclusion Technology Fund (FITF): The objective of FITF is to enhance investment in information and communication technology (ICT) aimed at promoting financial inclusion, stimulate the transfer of research and technology in financial inclusion, increase the technological absorption capacity of financial service providers/users and encourage an environment of innovation and cooperation among stakeholders.

A. Eligible Activities/Purposes: These are as follows:

1. Encouraging user-friendly technology solutions.

2. Providing financial support to technological solutions aimed at providing affordable financial services to the disadvantaged sections of the society.
3. Creating a common technology infrastructure with comprehensive credit information.
4. Funding support to technologies facilitating the documentation for processing of loans.
5. Providing viability gap/pilot project funding for unproven but potential technological interventions.
6. Conduct of studies, consultancies, research, evaluation studies relating to technological interventions for financial inclusion.
7. Promoting seminars, conferences and other mechanisms for discussions, dissemination relating to financial inclusion technological interventions.
8. Publication of financial inclusion technology literature, publicity material, etc.
9. Capacity building of personnel of banks, post offices, State Government Departments, MFIs, NGOs, and other stakeholders.
10. Any other activity as may be approved by the Advisory Board.

B. Eligible Institutions: These are as under:

1. Financial Institutions, viz. NABARD, commercial banks, regional rural banks (RRBs) and cooperative banks.
2. NGOs, MFIs, SHGs, farmers' clubs, local level associations etc.
3. Technology service providers and other service providers like insurance companies (providing micro insurance services), post offices, railways etc.
4. Any other institution/organisation whose objectives are in conformity with the overall objectives of the FITF and are approved by the advisory board.

To sum up, Indian economy in general and banking services in particular have made rapid strides in the recent past. However, a sizeable section of the population, particularly the vulnerable groups, such as weaker sections and low income groups, continue to remain excluded from even the most basic opportunities and services provided by the financial sector.

There are several challenges that require concerted efforts from banks, the RBI and the Government to ensure convenient and cost effective delivery of financial services to the public at large. In particular, the challenge is to introduce innovations in risk assessment, reduce transaction costs, devise new credit delivery channels, and use information technology to make financial inclusion a viable model.

2

Micro Credit, Self-help Groups (SHGs) and Support Agencies

The term *micro credit* did not exist before the 1970s. Now it has become a buzzword among the development practitioners. In the process, the term has been imputed to mean everything to everybody. No one now gets shocked if somebody uses the term micro credit to mean agricultural credit, or rural credit, or co-operative credit, or consumer credit, credit from the savings and loan associations, or from credit unions, or from money lenders.

Micro finance, a wider term, is the provision of thrift, credit and other financial services and products of very small amounts to the poor for enabling them to raise their income levels and improve their living standards. Thus, micro finance includes a range of financial services such as savings, credit, insurance etc. and the target group is poor and low income households.

2.1 UN Report on Micro Credit

The objective of the First United Nations Decade for the Eradication of Poverty (1997-2006), proclaimed by the General Assembly in its resolution 50/107 of December 20, 1995, is to achieve the goal of eradicating absolute poverty through national action and international cooperation.

The General Assembly, in its resolution 52/194 of December 18, 1997, noted that in many countries micro credit programmes have proved to be an effective tool in freeing people from poverty and have helped to increase their participation in the economic and political processes of society. Among other provisions, the Assembly called upon the relevant organs, organizations and bodies of the United

Nations system, in particular its funds and programmes and the regional commissions, as well as relevant international and regional financial institutions and donor agencies involved in the eradication of poverty, to explore including the micro credit approach in their programmes as a tool for the eradication of poverty. The assembly requested the Secretary-General, in collaboration with relevant organizations of the United Nations system, including funds and programmes and the World Bank, to submit to it at its fifty-third session a report on the role of micro credit in the eradication of poverty.

The World Summit for Social Development, held in Copenhagen in March 1995, also underlined the importance of improving access to credit for small rural or urban producers, landless farmers and other people with low or no income, with special attention to the needs of women and disadvantaged and vulnerable groups. Governments were called upon: (a) to review national legal, regulatory and institutional frameworks that restrict the access of people living in poverty, especially women, to credit on reasonable terms, (b) to promote realistic targets for access to affordable credit, (c) to provide incentives for improving access to and strengthening the capacity of organized credit systems to deliver credit and related services to people living in poverty and vulnerable groups, and (d) to expanding financial networks, building on existing networks, promoting attractive opportunities for savings and ensuring equitable access to credit at the local level.

2.2 Micro Credit for Equitable Growth

Several factors have led to increased interest in micro credit in promoting growth with greater equity. There has been a growth in the recognition of the importance of empowering all people by increasing their access to all the factors of production, including credit. In addition, the value of the role of non-governmental organizations in development is receiving more attention.

It is in that context that micro credit has recently assumed a certain degree of prominence. It is based on the recognition that the latent capacity of the poor for entrepreneurship would be encouraged with the availability of small-scale loans and would introduce them to the small-enterprise sector. This could allow them to be more self-reliant, create employment opportunities, and engage women in economically productive activities.

All economies rely upon the financial intermediary function to transfer resources from savers to investors. In market economies, this function is performed by commercial banks and the capital markets. More widespread financial intermediation is a hallmark of modern economy. But in many developing countries, capital markets are still at a rudimentary stage, and commercial banks are reluctant to lend to the poor largely because of the lack of collateral and high transaction costs. The poor would borrow relatively small amounts, and the processing and supervision of lending to them would consume administrative costs that would be disproportionate to the amount of lending.

Complicated loan procedures and paperwork, combined with a lack of accounting experience, limit poor people's access to formal sources of credit. Commercial lenders in rural areas prefer to deal mainly with large-scale farmers.

2.3 Credit Facilities for the Poor

Since independence, the Government of India and the RBI have made concerted efforts to provide the poor with access to credit. Despite the phenomenal increase in the physical outreach of formal credit institutions in the past several decades, the rural poor continue to depend on informal sources of credit. Institutions have also faced difficulties in dealing effectively with a large number of small borrowers, whose credit needs are small and frequent and their ability to offer collaterals is limited. Besides, cumbersome procedures and risk perceptions of the banks left a gap in serving the credit needs of the rural poor.

This led to a search for alternative policies, systems and procedures, saving and loan products, other complementary services and new delivery mechanisms that would fulfil the requirements of the poor. It is in this context that micro credit has emerged as the most suitable and practical alternative to the conventional banking in reaching the hitherto unreached poor population. Micro credit enables the poor people to be thrifty and helps them in availing the credit and other financial services for improving their income and living standards.

The proposed Micro Finance Services Regulation Bill defines micro finance services as providing financial assistance to an individual or an eligible client, either directly or through a group mechanism for an amount, not exceeding ₹ 50,000 in aggregate (₹ 1,50,000 if for housing purposes).

2.4 Micro Finance Initiative of National Bank for Agriculture and Rural Development (NABARD)

The micro finance initiative of NABARD, i.e. self-help groups (SHG)-Bank linkage programme has passed through various phases over the last one and half decades, *viz.* pilot testing during 1992 to 1995, mainstreaming during 1996 to 1998 and expansion from 1998 onwards.

Micro credit has emerged as a visible credit channel to the poor as their access to conventional credit channels is constrained by the requirement of collateral and high transaction cost. Micro finance is routed through SHGs. Over the years, SHG–Bank Linkage Programme—which includes commercial banks, regional rural banks and co-operative banks—has emerged as the major micro finance programme in the country. The focus under SHG-Bank Linkage Programme is largely on those rural poor who have no sustainable access to the formal banking system. The target groups, therefore, broadly comprise small and marginal farmers, agricultural and non-agricultural labourers, artisans and craftsmen and other poor engaged in small businesses like vending, and hawking.

The programme has been providing the rural poor access

to the formal banking system and has achieved several milestones in terms of gender sensitisation, empowerment and poverty alleviation. The programme provides thrift linked credit support to the members of SHGs. While the programme directly benefits the members, it also helps banks in reducing their transaction costs as well as risk in delivering small loans.

The programme has now assumed the form of a micro finance movement in many parts of the country and has started making inroads in the resource poor regions of the country as well.

SHG-Bank Linkage Programme was formally launched in the year 1992 as a flagship programme by NABARD and aptly supported by the RBI through its policy support. The objective is to meet the financial needs of the poor by linking SHGs with the formal credit agencies. The programme envisages organisation of the rural poor into SHGs for building their capacities to manage their own finances and then negotiate bank credit on commercial terms. The poor are encouraged to voluntarily come together to save small amounts regularly and extend micro loans among themselves. Once the group attains required maturity of handling larger resources, the bank credit follows.

A self-help group is a group of about 15 to 20 people from a homogenous class who join together to address common issues. They involve voluntary thrift activities on a regular basis, and use of the pooled resource to make interest-bearing loans to the members of the group. In the course of this process, they imbibe the essentials of financial intermediation and also the basics of account keeping. The members also learn to handle resources of size, much beyond their individual capacities. They begin to appreciate the fact that the resources are limited and have a cost.

Once the group is stabilised, and shows mature financial behaviour, which generally takes up to six months, it is considered for linking to banks. Banks are encouraged to provide loans to SHGs in certain multiples of the accumulated savings of the SHGs. Loans are given without any collateral and at interest rates as decided by banks. Banks find it comfortable to lend money to the groups as the members have already achieved some financial discipline through their thrift and internal lending activities. The groups decide the terms and conditions of loan to their own members. The peer pressure in the group ensures timely repayment and becomes social collateral for the bank loans.

2.5 Alternative Models of Micro Finance

India has adopted a multi-agency approach for the development of its micro finance programme. All the major credit institutions, *viz.* commercial banks, co-operative banks, RRBs along with non-governmental agencies (NGOs) have been associated with the micro finance programme. The role of the delivering agents and their interface has led to alternative models of micro finance.

Generally, the SHGs need self-help promoting institutions (SHPIs) to promote and nurture them. These SHPIs include various NGOs, banks, farmers' clubs, government agencies, self-employed individuals and federations of SHGs. However, some SHGs have also been formed without any assistance from such SHPIs.

Three distinct linkage models of micro credit are currently being followed in India.

Under Model-I, banks themselves take up the work of forming and nurturing the groups, opening their saving accounts and providing them bank loans.

Under Model-II, SHGs are formed by NGOs and formal agencies but are directly financed by banks.

Under Model-III, SHGs are financed by banks using NGOs and other agencies as financial intermediaries. In areas where formal banking system faces constraints, the NGOs are encouraged to approach suitable bank for bulk loan assistance.

2.6 Central Government and Micro Finance

It was announced in the Union Budget for 2005-06 that the

Government of India intends to promote micro finance institutions (MFIs) in a big way. For this purpose, the Micro-Finance Development Fund (MFDF) was re-designated as Micro-Finance Development and Equity Fund (MFDEF) and the corpus of the fund was increased from ₹ 100 crore to ₹ 200 crore. MFDEF is expected to play a vital role in capitalising the MFIs and thereby improving their access to commercial loans.

The Central Government is considering the need to identify and classify the MFIs and rate such institutions to empower them to intermediate between the lending banks and the clients. To facilitate the process of rating of MFIs, NABARD has decided to extend financial assistance to commercial banks and RRBs by way of grant to enable them to avail the services of credit rating agencies for rating of MFIs.

2.6.1 Micro Finance Development and Equity Fund (MFDEF): Recognising the need for up-scaling the micro finance interventions in the country, the Union Finance Minister, while presenting the budget for the year 2000-01, had created Micro Finance Development Fund (MFDF) with an initial contribution of ₹ 100 crore, to be funded by Reserve Bank of India, NABARD and commercial Banks in the ratio of 40:40:20. In the Union Budget for 2005-06, the Government of India decided to re-designate the MFDF into MFDEF and raised its corpus from ₹ 100 crore to ₹ 200 crore.

To strengthen the efforts of NABARD towards promotional support for micro finance, the Government of India in the Union Budget for 2010-11 further increased the corpus of MFDEF to ₹ 400 crore.

The MFDEF is managed and administered by NABARD under the guidance of an MFDEF Advisory Board. The objective of MFDEF is to facilitate and support the orderly growth of the micro finance sector through diverse modalities for enlarging the flow of financial services to the poor, particularly for women and vulnerable sections of society consistent with sustainability.

The Fund is utilised to support interventions to eligible institutions and stakeholders. The major components of the assistance include promotional grant assistance to self-help promoting agencies, training and capacity building for microfinance clients and stakeholders of SHG-Bank Linkage Programme, funding support to MFIs, management information system (MIS) for microfinance, research, studies and publications.

2.7 Reserve Bank of India (RBI) and Micro Finance

The RBI has been taking a pro-active role in promoting micro-finance. It set up four Groups in 2002 to look into various aspects of micro-financing. Based on the recommendations made by these Groups, the RBI announced that banks should provide adequate incentives to their branches in making the procedures for financing the SHGs simple and easy.

Based on the recommendations of the Vyas Committee, the RBI, in its annual policy statement for 2004-05, indicated that micro finance institutions would not be permitted to accept public deposits, unless they comply with the extant regulatory framework.

In view of the new paradigm shift in micro finance, the RBI is reviewing the issue of micro finance in a comprehensive manner. Accordingly, several initiatives have been taken in the recent period. A Technical Paper on Policy relating to Development, Regulation and Supervision of Micro finance Services was prepared and discussed with the representatives of MFIs on July 18, 2005. Similarly, an Internal Group of the RBI on Rural Credit and Micro-Finance (Chairman: H.R. Khan) was set up to examine the issues relating to micro-finance. The final version of the Report was released to the public in July 2005.

The SHG-Bank linkage programme is now considered by the banking system as a commercial proposition, with advantages of lower transaction cost, near zero NPAs and coverage of maximum number of the rural clientele by the bank branches. It has also led to other quantifiable benefits in business expansion. 27 commercial banks, 81 RRBs and 318 CCBs were participating in the programme at end-March 2010.

2.8 NABARD and Micro Credit

2.8.1 NABARD's Strategy for Popularity of Micro Finance: NABARD is adopting the following strategy to spread the outreach of SHG-Bank Linkage Programme.

1. Widening spatial distribution and intensity of the outreach of the Programme with district oriented planning and strategy.
2. Evolving district-wise plan of action/strategy in consultation with existing stakeholders aiming at promotion and linkage of a minimum of 500 SHGs per district every year.
3. Training and exposure programmes for the staff of the stakeholders.
4. Providing promotional assistance to partners for promoting and nurturing the SHGs generally on an *add-on* basis.
5. Widening the range of SHG promoting agencies.
6. Involving banks at their corporate level, organising training programmes for the regional/zonal managers of commercial banks in association with their Central Offices.
7. Establishing the financing of SHGs as a business proposition for banks.
8. Increasing the participation of the co-operative banks by encouraging them to finance SHGs as *financing co-operatives within the co-operatives*.
9. Associating village communities, people's institutions, rural volunteers and individuals to participate in the programme as SHG promoters.
10. Increasing the quality of the existing SHGs by propagating *self-rating* tools.

11. Large-scale dissemination of the concept and approach among the rural masses.
12. Encouraging the NGOs to play an important role in correcting the regional imbalances in spread of SHG-Bank Linkage Programme.

2.8.2 Tracking the Progress of Micro Finance: In view of the large outreach and pre-dominant position of the micro finance programme, it is important to keep a continuous track of the status, progress, trends, qualitative and quantitative performance comprehensively. To achieve this objective, Reserve Bank of India and NABARD issued guidelines in the year 2006-07 to commercial banks, regional rural banks and co-operative banks to furnish data on progress under micro finance. The data so collected covers various parameters like savings of SHGs with banks, bank loan disbursed to SHGs, bank loan outstanding against SHGs, gross non-performing assets of bank loans to SHGs, recovery performance of loans to SHGs. Further, the banks also furnish the data regarding bank loans provided to micro finance institutions (MFIs). NABARD, has been bringing out the consolidated document annually.

The data furnished by the banks have been analysed on a region-wise, state-wise, agency-wise, bank-wise and also for SHGs exclusively under Swarnajayanti Gram Swarojgar Yojana and exclusive women SHGs.

The major support provided by NABARD under Micro Finance Development and Equity Fund relates to promotion and nurturing of SHGs by self-help promoting institutions and training and capacity building of the stakeholders in the sector. NABARD is also experimenting innovative projects for further developing the micro finance through joint liability groups.

Since 2006-07, NABARD has been compiling and analysing the data on progress made in micro finance sector, based on the returns furnished by commercial banks (CBs), regional rural banks (RRBs) and co-operative banks operating in the country. The banks operating, presently, in the formal financial system comprises public sector CBs (26), private sector CBs (20), RRBs (64), state co-operative banks (31) and district central co-operative banks (372). Most of the banks participating in the process of microfinance have reported the progress made under the programme.

NABARD has been instrumental in facilitating various activities under micro finance sector, involving all possible partners at the ground level in the field. NABARD has been encouraging voluntary agencies, bankers, socially spirited individuals, other formal and informal entities and also government functionaries to promote and nurture SHGs. The focus in this direction has been on training and capacity building of partners, promotional grant assistance to self-help promoting institutions (SHPIs), Revolving Fund Assistance (RFA) to MFIs, equity/capital support to MFIs to supplement their financial resources and provision of 100 percent refinance against bank loans provided by various banks for microfinance activities.

2.8.3 Micro Enterprise Development Programme (MEDP) for Skill Development: MEDP was launched by NABARD in March 2006 with the basic objective to enhance the capacities of the members of matured SHGs to take up micro enterprises through appropriate skill upgradation/development in the existing or new livelihood activities both in farm and non-farm sectors by way of enriching knowledge of participants on enterprise management, business dynamics and rural markets. It is tailor-made and focused on skill building training programme. The duration of training programme ranged between 3 and 13 days, depending upon the objective and nature of training.

The dominant activities in agriculture and allied sector covered under MEDPs were animal husbandry, bee-keeping, mushroom cultivation, vermicompost/organic manure, horticulture, floriculture, etc. whereas predominant non-farm activities taken up under MEDPs were readymade garments, agarbatti-making, embroidery, bamboo-craft, beauty parlours, etc.

2.8.4 Support to Activity-based Groups: NABARD introduced a scheme for supporting small-scale activity based groups (ABGs) in 2008-09, wherein capacity building, production and investment credit and market-related support would be extended. The scheme focuses on forming and nurturing the groups engaged in similar economic activities, such as farmers, handloom weavers, craftsmen, fishermen, etc., to improve efficiency of their production and realise better terms from the market through economies of aggregation and scale. The scheme drew upon NABARD's existing modes of support and has both grant and loan components. While grant support covers expenditure on SHGs formation and training, extension services, establishing market linkages, etc. bank loan/s would cover investment activities and working capital needs of the SHGs. Banks are eligible to draw refinance for the loans provided to Activity-based Groups on the same terms as applicable for SHG's financing. In select cases, NABARD provides loans directly to registered SHGs or through the agencies promoting SHGs to establish few initial projects where none exists.

2.8.5 Support to Federations of SHGs: Recognising the emerging role of the SHGs' Federations in nurturing of SHGs, enhancing the bargaining powers of group members and livelihood promotion, NABARD introduced during 2007-08, a flexible scheme to support such Federations, irrespective of their model. The broad norms prescribed for supporting SHG Federations stipulate that the federations should be need-based, member-owned/driven, democratically managed with members at liberty to join, become self-managed over three years, etc. NABARD extends grant support to the Federation for training, capacity building, and exposure visits of SHG members, etc., as also under all of NABARD's existing promotional schemes.

2.8.6 Centre for Micro Finance Research: With the funding support from MFDEF, a Centre for Micro finance Research (CMR) has been setup in Bankers Institute of Rural

Development, Lucknow to take up research studies in the field of microfinance with the mission of strengthening microfinance sector through supply of research inputs to facilitate policy initiatives and improvements in design and delivery system that provide poor with sustainable access to quality financial services. The CMR along with four sub-centres viz., Indian Institute of Bank Management (IIBM), Guwahati, Institute of Financial Management and Research (IFMR), Chennai, Institute of Development Studies (IDS), Jaipur and Chadragupta Institute of Management, Patna (CIMP) had initiated several studies on critical issues of microfinance. Grant assistance of ₹ 375 lakh was sanctioned to CMR from MFDEF to pursue the above-envisaged activities.

2.8.7 Joint Liability Groups (JLGs): Based on the studies conducted by NABARD, it was found that financing of JLGs is a good business proposition. It needs simplified documentation, group dynamics, timely repayment culture and prospects of credit enhancement to quality clients. Keeping in view the need and findings of the studies, NABARD has issued comprehensive guidelines on JLGs to Banks focusing on small and marginal farmers, oral lessees, tenant farmers engaged in farm sector and other clients under non-farm activities. NABARD supports banks for nurturing and financing of JLGs for the initial three years. Banks may use the services of JLG-promoting agencies. In addition, NABARD would also extend support for training, exposure visits, experience-sharing, etc., for banks' staff.

SHG-Bank linkage programme has proved to be successful in providing financial services from the formal banking sector to the poor. However, the issue of linking the small/marginal farmers, tenant farmers/oral lessees, share croppers and the rural non-farm entrepreneurs with the formal banking sector was concern for NABARD as their demand were not met through the SHG as in SHGs, loan amount is linked to savings. NABARD had piloted joint liability groups (JLGs) programme during 2004-05 in eight states of the country with the help of

13 RRBs through the mechanism of joint liability approach. Besides the above pilot project, the Government of Andhra Pradesh through its Agriculture Department primarily designed the initiative by promoting Rythu Mithra Groups (RMGs) on the SHG model.

RMGs are also expected to serve as a conduit for technology transfer, facilitate access to market information and assist in carrying out activities like soil testing, training, health camps, assess input requirements, etc., to its members.

Over the last few years NABARD has been propagating the idea of JLGs at various fora. Based on the experience gained in implementation of the pilot project, a scheme for financing JLGs by the commercial banks, RRBs and co-operative banks has been formulated and circulated to RRBs and Co-operative Banks by NABARD and to commercial banks through Reserve Bank of India/Indian Banks Association.

2.9 Recommendations of the Group on Rural Credit and Micro Finance, 2005

As a follow-up to the announcement in the Union Budget, 2005-06, the RBI constituted this Internal Group (Chairman: H.R. Khan) which in its Report submitted in July 2005 observed that there is an imperative need to work out efficient mechanisms involving external entities to cater to the under-serviced areas and the rural poor.

The Group felt that extended outreach to the under-serviced areas and the rural poor would facilitate acquisition of a large number of customers, *albeit* small ones with substantial potential for large increase in business volumes and profit as banking with the poor is rather profitable banking. The major recommendations of the Group are set out below.

1. For providing comprehensive financial services encompassing savings, credit and remittance, insurance and pension products in rural areas, the Group recommended two models, *viz.*, the Business Facilitator Model and the Business

Correspondent Model as proactive response.

2. Under the Business Facilitator Model, it was envisaged that banks could use a wide array of civil society organisations (CSOs) and others for supporting them by undertaking non-financial services. The Facilitators would provide support services for effective delivery of financial services such as: (a) borrower identification, (b) collection, processing and submission of applications, (c) preliminary appraisal, (c) marketing of the financial products including savings, (d) post-sanction monitoring, (e) promotion and nurturing SHGs/joint liability groups (JLGs), and (f) follow-up for recovery.
3. NGOs, farmers clubs, functional co-operatives, IT enabled rural outlets of corporates, postal agents, insurance agents, well-functioning panchayats, rural multi-purpose kiosks/village knowledge centres, agri-clinics/business centres financed by banks, *krishi vigyan kendras*, Khadi and Village Industry Commission (KVIC)/Khadi and Village Industries Commission Board (KVIB) units may function as the Business Facilitators.
4. Under the Business Correspondent Model, institutional agents/other external entities may support the banks for extending financial services. The Business Correspondents would function as "pass through" agencies to provide credit related services such as disbursal of small value credit, recovery of principal/ collection of interest and sale of micro insurance/mutual fund products/pension products besides the other functions of Business Facilitator Model.
5. Registered NBFCs with significant rural presence, NGO-micro finance institutions (MFIs) set up under the Societies/Trust Act, mutually aided co-operative societies (MACS) with a charter to undertake financial functions, IT enabled rural outlets of corporates with appropriate contractual agreements with the principal, well running primary agricultural credit societies (PACSs) and post offices may function as the Business Correspondents.

6. The micro credit portfolio of the regulated MFIs may be made eligible for direct finance from NABARD; a line of credit may be extended by NABARD to provide liquidity assistance in view of the co-variant nature of credit risk of the MFIs.
7. Institutions such as NABARD and SIDBI may provide bulk lending support to start-up MFIs and funds of State/ Central Development/Finance Corporations, if feasible, may be channelised through NABARD to identified MFIs.
8. Accounting standards for SHGs and NGOs may be developed, codified, and standardised by NABARD as a promotional initiative in consultation with the Institute of Chartered Accountants of India (ICAI).
9. NABARD, in consultation with Ministry of Information and Technology, may draw up a time bound action plan to set up rural kiosks/village knowledge centres, partly funded from RIDF. The remaining cost may be borne by the Central/State Governments on a shared basis.
10. The MFIs may be rated to help banks/financial institutions to decide about engaging them as their agents and funding them. The rating agencies need to be accredited with an appropriate authority.
11. NABARD, SIDBI and major banks may consider promoting independent rating agencies by way of equity contributions. Financial support may be provided to the accredited rating agencies to cover their operational deficits for a period of three to five years and the expenses in this regard may be met from the Micro Finance Development and Equity Fund (MFDEF).
12. Non-deposit taking MFIs may attempt self-regulation by forming State level associations.
13. A separate and exclusive regulatory and supervisory framework for MFIs may not be required for the present.
14. Considering the high transaction costs and the emphasis on timely availability of credit, it may not be appropriate to fix any ceiling on interest rates and service fees charged by MFIs.

2.10 Challenges for Future

Over the past decade, micro finance institutions have adopted innovative ways of providing credit and savings services to the entrepreneurial poor. Two approaches have been advocated on the role of credit in poverty reduction. While supporters of the *income-generation approach* maintain that credit should be provided mainly to the entrepreneurial poor to enable them to finance specific private income-generating activities to increase their revenues, proponents of the so-called *minimalist approach* argue that credit progammes would still be helping the poor fight poverty by giving credit to any poor person who is able to repay a loan without dictating to that person how and on what the loan should be used. Some studies have pointed out that the problem of the non-productive use of credit, as advocated by the minimalist approach, lies in the fact that by consuming rather than investing their loans, the actions of such borrowers, if imitated by other poor people, could produce a negative impact on the future growth of micro credit.

Several micro finance institutions have succeeded in reaching the poorest of the poor by devising innovative strategies. These include the provision of small loans to poor people, especially in rural areas, at full-cost interest rates, without collateral, that are repayable in frequent instalments. Borrowers are organized into groups, which reduces the risk of default. These are also effective mechanisms through which to disseminate valuable information on ways to improve the health, legal rights, sanitation and other relevant concerns of the poor. Above all, many micro credit programmes have targeted one of the most vulnerable groups in society, i.e. women who live in households that own little or no assets. By providing opportunities for self-employment, many studies have concluded that these programmes have significantly increased women's security, autonomy, self-confidence and status within the household.

Targeting is a particularly thorny topic. There have been

allegations that in fact the very poor are so weak as not to benefit from micro lending, and that it is the *better off poor* that benefit. While all the poor need to be included in the programmes, the shortage of funds impels organizers to make special efforts to reach the less well-off among the poor. Micro credit should be viewed as complementary to the provision of basic services like education, housing, health and nutrition. The latter are indispensable in the fight against poverty.

A crucial part of any future effort should be to strengthen the administrative structures of existing micro credit institutions proliferate. It is possible that economies of scale are important in micro lending. Dynamic leadership and paid management staff are probably crucial. The provision of information on available services to the poor is particularly essential. This is not at present the case, even in some advanced developing countries. Information on services for the poor is rarely made readily available.

In that context, the long-term financial sustainability of micro credit operations deserves particular attention. In the more successful schemes, repayment rates are high, but this is not so with many operations that do not have a high profile. In the absence of long-term sustainability, micro credit operations become a welfare or charity operation. While the latter have their own place in development in some circumstances, they should not characterize micro credit institutions.

Probably the single most important element in ensuring long-term sustainability of these operations is to include in them the savings mobilization function. This is not always the case at the present time. The operation that lends to the poor should also cater to their savings needs. In many developing countries, savings habits are quite widespread, but the institutional structures do not usually cater to them. The possibility of combining savings and lending operations in some form of credit union organization should always be explored.

To sum up, the micro credit programme, which was

formally heralded in 1992 with a modest pilot project of linking around 500 self-help groups (SHGs), has made rapid strides in India exhibiting considerable democratic functioning and group dynamism. The micro credit programme in India is now the largest in the world. Since Independence, the Government of India and the RBI have made concerted efforts to provide the poor with access to credit. Despite the phenomenal increase in the physical outreach of formal credit institutions in the past several decades, the rural poor continue to depend on informal sources of credit. Institutions have also faced difficulties in dealing effectively with a large number of small borrowers, whose credit needs are small and frequent and their ability to offer collaterals is limited. Besides, cumbersome procedures and risk perceptions of the banks left a gap in serving the credit needs of the rural poor.

It should be noted that although a large number of studies undertaken so far on the impact of micro credit programmes on household income show that participants of such programmes usually have higher and more stable incomes than they did before they joined the programmes, some practitioners still have reservations about the findings of these studies. Moreover, not many micro credit programmes can afford to undertake impact assessments because they are generally expensive and time-consuming. There are serious disagreements among experts on the validity of methodologies used in some of the published studies. In some cases, even the more rigorous studies have produced inconclusive results. Some studies show that there are limits to the use of credit as an instrument for poverty eradication, including difficulties in identifying the poor and targeting credit to reach the poorest of the poor. Added to this is the fact that many people, especially the poorest of the poor, are usually not in a position to undertake an economic activity, partly because they lack business skills and even the motivation for business.

If micro credit is to play a strong role in development, certain requirements need to be fulfilled. The most crucial requirement is to perceive micro credit lending as part of a comprehensive programme of support to the small enterprise sector.

This would entail Governments of developing countries formulating plans and programmes to support small enterprises in general, of which micro credit should be an integral part. Furthermore, the regulatory framework should be receptive to small enterprises. Many micro borrowers have complained of this particular shortcoming in developing countries.

3

Rural Co-operative Banks in India

Historically, rural co-operative credit institutions (or simply rural co-operatives) have played an important role in providing institutional credit to the agricultural and rural sectors. The structure of rural co-operative banks is not uniform across all the States of the country. Some States have a unitary structure with the State level banks operating through their own branches, while others have a mixed structure incorporating both unitary and federal systems.

3.1 Credit and Agricultural Development

Being the backbone of the Indian economy, agriculture has all along been treated as a priority sector for the allocation of institutional credit. The low growth rate of agriculture in the past few years has further strengthened the channels of credit flow to this sector.

Agricultural production in India depends upon millions of small farmers. It is the intensity of their effort and the efficiency of their technique that will help in raising yields per acre. Because of inadequate financial resources and absence of timely credit facilities at reasonable rates, many of the farmers, even though otherwise willing, are unable to go in for improved seeds and manures or to introduce better methods or techniques. It is, therefore, of the utmost importance that the financial requirements of the farmers are adequately met.

Provision of sufficient and timely credit at fair rates of interest has, therefore, to be considered as an integral part of agricultural development. Assistance rendered by way of credit has, however, to be related to specific items of productive work or of essential costs of cultivation. Following guidelines from the RBI, commercial banks are increasingly devoting attention to agricultural sector to meet its credit needs.

Agricultural growth is crucial for alleviating rural poverty. Access to institutional credit to more farmers and appropriate quantity and quality of agricultural credit are crucial for realising the full potential of agriculture as a profitable activity.

The Government has taken many policy initiatives for strengthening farm credit delivery system for providing credit at affordable rates of interest to support the resource requirements of the agricultural sector. The emphasis of these initiatives has been on providing timely and adequate credit support to farmers with particular focus on small and marginal farmers and weaker sections of society to enable them to adopt modern technology and improved agricultural practices for increasing agricultural production and productivity. The policy essentially lays emphasis on augmenting credit flow at the ground level through credit planning, adoption of region specific strategies and rationalization of lending policies and procedures and bringing down the rate of interest on farm loan.

3.2 Credit Needs of the Indian Farmers

Need for agricultural credit arises because modern farm technology is costly and the personal resources of the farmers are inadequate. Provision of agricultural credit, as an input, is essential for widespread use of improved agricultural methods. Credit requirements of the farmers may be classified: (a) on the basis of purpose, and (b) on the basis of time. They need credit for productive as well as for unproductive purposes. Productive purposes include all such activities which help in the improvement of agricultural productivity such as purchase of inputs and permanent improvements in land. Unproductive credit needs include celebration of marriages and other social and religious functions and litigation.

Finance required for productive purposes can be divided broadly into the following categories:

- Short-term (for periods up to 15 months).

- Medium-term (from 15 months up to 5 years).
- Long-term (above 5 years).

Short-term loans are required for purchasing seeds, manures and fertilizers or for meeting labour charges etc. These are expected to be repaid after the harvest.

Medium-term loans are granted for purposes such as sinking of wells, purchase of bullocks, pumping plants and other improved implements etc.

Loans repayable over a longer period (*i.e.* above 5 years) are classified as long-term loans. These are utilised for payment of old debts, purchase of the heavier machines, making permanent improvements and increasing the size of the holding.

3.3 Sources of Credit for the Farmers

Sources of agricultural credit are grouped into two categories: (a) institutional sources, and (b) non-institutional sources. Institutional sources include co-operative societies, commercial banks and other government agencies. Non-institutional sources comprise moneylenders, landlords, relatives etc.

Till Independence in 1947, money lenders and the landlords were the principal sources of rural credit. Over the years, the operations of moneylenders have declined in view of debt relief legislations, the system of licensing moneylenders and restrictions on the use and transfer of land as security. Similarly, the abolition of all privileged tenures, both in zamindari and ryotwari areas, has discouraged investment by the landlords and larger cultivators.

3.3.1 Institutional Arrangements: Agricultural credit is disbursed through a multi-agency network comprising of commercial banks, regional rural banks and co-operatives. With their vast network (covering almost all the villages in the country), wider coverage and outreach extending to the remotest part of country, the co-operative credit institutions, both in short and long-term structure are the main institutional mechanism for dispensation of agricultural credit.

3.3.2 Moneylenders: It is true that the institutional sources of credit have weakened the hold of moneylenders on the rural masses. However, the benefits of institutional credit have not percolated to all sections of rural population. Landless workers and marginal farmers have not benefited adequately due to their ignorance of new sources of credit and also on account of their weak repaying capacity. These underprivileged rural sections still depend on the moneylenders and suffer their exploitative practices.

Historically, moneylenders have played a significant role in meeting the credit needs of the rural producers. With stringent laws against money lending and the phenomenal growth of the formal credit delivery system, it was thought that money lenders would soon be out of business. Instead they have been in the business of lending in several disguises.

There are two types of moneylenders in rural areas: (a) agriculturist moneylenders who carry on the business of money lending along with farming, and (b) professional moneylenders whose only occupation is money lending. Although the relative importance of moneylenders has declined over the years, they are still an important source of credit for the rural people, particularly the small farmers and the artisans.

Moneylenders are popular because, unlike government agencies, they give credit for every purpose. They are easily approachable by the credit seekers and there are not many formalities in transacting a loan. However, the malpractices adopted by the moneylenders to exploit the needy farmers cannot be overlooked. These malpractices pertain to charging of high rate of interest and adopting unfair means in the maintenance of accounts.

Agricultural growth is crucial for alleviating rural poverty. Access to institutional credit to more farmers and appropriate quantity and quality of agricultural credit are crucial for realising the full potential of agriculture as a profitable activity.

Provision of sufficient and timely credit at fair rates of interest has, therefore, to be considered as an integral part of agricultural development. Assistance rendered by way of credit has, however, to be related to specific items of productive work or of essential costs of cultivation.

3.4 Co-operative Credit Societies

These societies form an integral part of the rural credit system in India. They are the main source of institutional credit to the farmers. These societies are chiefly responsible for breaking the monopoly of moneylenders in providing credit to the agriculturists. There are around 1 lakh such societies in the country at present. In spite of their suitability and useful role in building up a just socio-economic rural life, co-operative societies suffer from various weaknesses. The heavy overdues of co-operative societies are a cause for concern. The rising overdues have reduced the borrowing and lending activities of these societies. Moreover, these societies have paid inadequate attention to the needs of landless workers and rural artisans. Influential people in the villages have been the main beneficiaries of co-operative credit. Of late, there has been a tendency on the part of political leadership to write-off loans of the farmers. The RBI has repeatedly expressed concern in this regard because non-repayment of loans by the existing borrowers can adversely affect recycling of funds and the credit chances of the prospective borrowers.

3.5 Co-operative Banks

Co-operative banks in India are more than 100 years old. These banks came into existence with the enactment of the Agricultural Credit Co-operative Societies Act in 1904. Co-operative banks form an integral part of the banking system in India. These banks operate mainly for the benefit of rural areas, particularly the agricultural sector. Co-operative banks mobilise deposits and supply agricultural and rural credit with a wider outreach. They are the main source of institutional credit to the farmers. Co-operative banks are chiefly responsible for breaking the monopoly of moneylenders in providing credit to agriculturists. They have also been an important instrument for various development schemes, particularly subsidy-based programmes for the poor. Co-operative banks operate for non-agricultural sector also but their role is small.

Though much smaller as compared to scheduled commercial banks, co-operative banks constitute an important segment of the Indian banking system. They have an extensive branch network and reach out to people in remote areas. They have traditionally played an important role in creating banking habits among the lower and middle-income groups and in strengthening the rural credit delivery system.

The financial reforms process initiated in 1991 has tried to achieve regulatory convergence among various financial intermediaries in view of their systemic importance. Therefore, the basic objectives and instruments of reforms for co-operative banks have been the same as for State Co-operative Banks (SCBs). However, given the special characteristics of co-operative banks, they have been extended certain dispensations in terms of pace and sequencing of reforms.

3.5.1 Classification of Co-operative Banks: The co-operative banking structure in India comprises urban co-operative banks and rural co-operative credit institutions.

A. Urban Co-operative Banks (UCBs): UCBs consist of a single tier, *viz.* primary co-operative banks, commonly referred to as urban co-operative banks.

B. Rural Co-operatives: Based on the nature of their lending operations, rural credit co-operatives have traditionally been bifurcated into two parallel wings: short-term and long-term.

3.6 Rural Co-operatives

3.6.1 Short-term Rural Co-operatives: The short-term provide crop and other working capital loans to farmers and rural artisans primarily for short-term purposes. These credit institutions have a three-tier federal structure: (a) At the apex of the system is a State Co-operative Bank (SCB) in each State; (b) At the middle (or district) level, there are Central Co-operative Banks (CCBs) also known as district co-operative banks; and (c) At the lowest (or village) level are the Primary Agricultural Credit Societies (PACS). The smaller States and Union Territories (UTs) have a two-tier structure with SCBs directly meeting the credit requirements of PACS.

A. State Co-operative Bank (SCB): SCB is the highest agency of the three-tier co-operative credit structure in a state. It serves as a link between RBI and the CCBs and PACS. The RBI provides credit to lower level co-operatives through the SCB. This function of the RBI has now been taken over by NABARD. The SCB also acts as a *balancing centre* for CCBs in the sense that surplus funds of some CCBs are made available to other needy CCBs. The SCB exercises general control and supervision over CCBs and PACS.

B. Central Co-operative Banks (CCBs): These banks act as a link between the SCB and the PACS. The main task of CCBs is to lend money to affiliated village primary societies. The CCBs are expected to attract deposits from the general public.

C. Primary Agricultural Credit Societies (PACS): These societies form the basic unit of the co-operative credit system in India. These voluntary societies based on the principle of one man one vote have posed challenge to the exploitative practices of the village moneylenders.

The farmers and other small-time borrowers come in direct contact with these societies. The success of the co-operative credit movement depends largely on the strength of these village level societies. There are around 1 lakh such societies in the country at present.

As a result of the expansion of the activities of PACS, the role of moneylenders in providing credit to agriculturists has decreased over the years. A major objective of PACS is to serve the needs of weaker sections of the society. For this purpose, the people with limited means, particularly scheduled castes and scheduled tribes, are encouraged to become members of these societies. Government has promoted multi-purpose societies in tribal areas for the benefit of people living there.

3.6.2 Long-term Rural Co-operatives: The long-term provide typically medium and long-term loans for making investments in agriculture, rural industries and, in the recent period, housing. Generally, these co-operatives have two tiers, *viz.*

A. State Co-operative Agriculture and Rural Development Banks (SCARDBs): These banks operate at the State level.

B. Primary Co-operative Agriculture and Rural Development Banks (PCARDBs): These banks operate at the *taluka/tehsil* level.

3.7 Rural Co-operatives: History and Recent Policy Measures

Rural credit co-operatives in India were originally envisaged as a mechanism for pooling the resources of people with small means and providing them with access to different financial services. Democratic in features, the movement was also an effective instrument for development of degraded waste lands, increasing productivity, providing food security, generating employment opportunities in rural areas and ensuring social and economic justice to the poor and vulnerable.

The history of the co-operative credit movement in India can be traced back to 1904 when the Co-operative Societies Act was passed. In 1919, *co-operation* became a provincial subject. The Co-operative Planning Committee, 1945 found that a large number of co-operatives were "saddled with the problem of frozen assets because of heavy overdues in repayment."

The co-operative banks in India play an important role in catering to the banking needs of the rural population. Soon after Independence in 1947, the inadequacy of rural credit engaged the attention of the Government of India and the RBI. The agricultural credit system as it has emerged over the years is the result of both evolution and intervention, and symbolises the nation's response to the dissatisfaction with the discredited colonial credit delivery system.

The Reserve Bank of India Act, 1934 has specific provisions relating to agricultural credit. Section 54 of the RBI Act specifically authorised the creation of an Agricultural Credit Department within the RBI to deal not only with the rural credit but also with the long-term finance including refinance. Section 17 of the Act empowered it to provide agricultural credit through state co-operative banks or any other banks engaged in the business of agricultural credit.

The foundation for building a broader credit infrastructure for rural credit was laid down by the All India Rural Credit Survey (1954). The Committee of Direction that conducted the survey recommended the creation of National Agricultural Credit Fund, which was subsequently created by the RBI. The Agricultural Refinance Corporation (ARC) set up by the RBI in 1963 provided funds by way of refinance, but credit co-operatives still did not function too well. Decentralised credit planning through the Lead Bank Scheme was also introduced to spearhead the credit allocation for, *inter alia*, agricultural lending. In order to emphasise the developmental and promotional role assigned to the ARC in addition to refinancing, the ARC was renamed as the Agricultural Refinance and Development Corporation (ARDC) in 1975.

Despite all these efforts, the flow of credit to the agricultural sector failed to exhibit any appreciable improvement as the co-operatives lacked resources to meet the expected demand. To solve these problems, the regional rural banks (RRBs) were set up in 1975. In order to strengthen the institutional credit for agriculture and rural development, National Bank for Agriculture and Rural Development (NABARD) was set up on July 12, 1982. On its establishment, NABARD took over the entire functions of the ARDC, the refinancing functions of the RBI in relation to co-operatives and regional rural banks (RRBs).

The rural credit co-operative system has served as an important instrument of credit delivery in rural and agricultural areas. The separate structure of rural co-operative sector for long-term and short-term loans has enabled these institutions to develop as specialised institutions for rural credit delivery. At the same time, their federal structure has helped in providing support structure for the guidance and critical financing for the lower structure. These institutions have wide outreach with as many as 93,413 primary agricultural co-operative societies (PACS), the grass root organisation of the rural co-operative banking structure with over 9 crore members, operating in the country as on March 31, 2013.

The rural co-operative credit institutions, however, are beset with many problems which include the following.

1. Low resource base.
2. High dependence on refinancing agencies.
3. Lack of diversification.
4. Huge accumulated losses.
5. Persistent NPAs.
6. Low recovery levels.
7. Various other types of organisational weaknesses.

NABARD and the RBI, therefore, have been taking several supervisory and developmental measures in consultation with the Government of India for the revival of weak institutions and orderly growth of this important segment of the financial sector.

3.8 Primary Agricultural Credit Societies (PACS)

Primary agricultural credit societies (PACS) are the foundation of the co-operative credit system on which the superstructure of the short-term co-operative credit system rests. It is the PACS which directly interface with individual farmers, provide short-term and medium-term credit, supply agricultural inputs, distribute consumer articles and arrange for marketing of produce of its members through a co-operative marketing society.

PACS continue to rely heavily on external support and have not yet been able to become self-reliant in respect of resources through deposit mobilisation and internal accruals, affecting their growth and expansion of business activities.

PACS need to function as viable units responsive to the needs, aspirations and convenience of its members, particularly those belonging to the more vulnerable sections of the society. They must function effectively as well-managed and multi-purpose institutions mobilising the savings of the rural people and providing a package of services including credit, supply of agricultural inputs and implements, consumer goods, marketing services and technical guidance with focus on weaker sections.

Some of the critical challenges facing primary level co-operative credit institutions, apart from improving resource mobilisation, are the following.

- Increasing diversification in business portfolio.
- Improving volume of business.
- Arresting decline in membership by the borrowers.
- Reducing cost of management.
- Correcting imbalances in loans outstanding.
- Improving skills of the staff and imparting professionalisation.
- Strengthening management information system (MIS).
- Reducing involvement in non/less profitable business.

3.9 NABARD and the Co-operative Sector

National Bank for Agriculture and Rural Development (NABARD) provides refinance to state co-operative agriculture and rural development banks (SCARDBs), state co-operative banks (SCBs), regional rural banks (RRBs) and other financial institutions approved by the RBI. The ultimate beneficiaries of refinance from NABARD could be individuals, partnership concerns, companies, State-owned corporations or co-operative societies.

3.9.1 Credit Extended by NABARD: NABARD provides short-term credit facilities to SCBs in respect of eligible CCBs for the following purposes:

- Financing seasonal agricultural operations.
- Marketing of crops.
- Pisciculture activities.
- Production and marketing activities of primary weavers/other industrial co-operative societies.
- Labour contract/forest labour co-operative societies.
- Individual rural artisans through PCS.
- Procurement, stocking and distribution of chemical fertilisers.
- Approved agricultural, allied and other marketing activities.

Besides short-term credit limits are also sanctioned to SCBs on behalf of apex/regional weavers/other industrial societies for financing procurement and marketing and trading-in-yarn.

Short-term limits are also provided to RRBs for financing seasonal agricultural operations, marketing of crops and pisciculture activities. Medium-term facilities are also provided to SCBs and RRBs for converting short-term into medium-term loans and for approved agricultural investments. Long-term loans are provided to the State Governments for contributing to the share capital of co-operative credit institutions.

In pursuance of the announcement made by the Finance Minister in June 2004 for enhancing the credit flow to the agriculture sector, NABARD advised SCBs, CCBs and RRBs on the measures to be taken under various schemes to give relief to farmers. It was apprehended that the implementation of these measures coupled with providing conversion/rescheduled loans to farmers may result in a liquidity problem for co-operative banks and RRBs, impairing their ability to provide fresh loans and achieve the desired growth rate during the year. In order to mitigate this, NABARD introduced a liquidity support scheme during 2004-05 for these institutions. SCBs were sanctioned a liquidity support of ₹ 1,770 crore during 2004-05. NABARD also sanctioned long-term loans to 9 State Governments amounting to ₹ 39 crore as contribution to the share capital of co-operative credit institutions.

3.10 Regulatory Framework and Supervision

3.10.1 Asset Classification for State Government Guaranteed Advances: Revised guidelines on asset classification norms for State Government guaranteed exposures (i.e. advances and investments), as applicable to commercial banks, were issued to SCBs and CCBs on January 20, 2005 which are to be implemented in a phased manner. Accordingly, it was decided to delink the asset classification and provisioning requirements in respect of State Government guaranteed loans and advances from invocation of State Government guarantee and treat such exposures for asset classification purpose in the same manner as applicable to exposures not guaranteed by the State Governments. However, with a view to enabling banks to have a smooth transition in the matter, the revised prudential norms in respect of State Government guaranteed exposures (*i.e.* both advances and investments) will be implemented in a phased manner in two stages.

With effect from the year ending March 31, 2006, State Government guaranteed advances and investments in State Government guaranteed securities would attract asset classification and provisioning norms, if interest and/or instalment of principal or any other amount due to the bank remains overdue for more than 180 days. In the second stage, which would begin from the year ending March 31, 2007, State Government guaranteed advance and investment in State Government guaranteed securities would attract asset classification and provisioning norms, if interest and/or instalment of principal or any other amount due to the bank remains overdue for more than 90 days.

3.10.2 Additional Provisioning Requirement for NPAs: For the sake of convergence in policies governing all banks, guidelines for additional provisioning for all advances classified as *doubtful for more than three years* were issued on March 01, 2005, to be implemented in a phased manner from April 01, 2007. In terms of the guidelines, for the unsecured portion of the advance, which is not covered by the realisable value of tangible security to which the bank has a valid recourse and the realisable value is estimated on a realistic basis, provision will be to the extent of 100 percent, as hitherto. The secured portion, on the other hand, would be divided into two categories. Outstanding stock of NPAs classified as *doubtful for more than three years* as on March 31, 2007 would need to be provided for in a phased manner up to 100 percent till March 31, 2010. Also, 100 percent provisioning would need to be made for the advances classified as *doubtful for more than three years* on or after April 1, 2007.

3.10.3 Prudential Guidelines on Agricultural Advances: As mentioned in the Annual Policy Statement of the RBI for the year 2004-05, prudential norms on income recognition, asset classification and provisioning with respect to agricultural advances were modified on July 12, 2004 with a view to aligning the repayment dates with harvesting of crops. Accordingly, effective September 30, 2004 a loan granted for short duration crops is required to be treated as NPA if the instalment of the principal or interest thereon remains unpaid for two crop seasons beyond the due date. A loan granted for long duration (with crop season longer than one year) crops is required to be treated as NPA, if the instalment of principal or interest thereon remains unpaid for one crop season beyond the due date.

3.10.4 Inspections: NABARD undertakes inspection of RRBs, SCBs and CCBs in accordance with the powers vested under Section 35(6) of the Banking Regulation Act, 1949

(AACS). Besides, NABARD conducts voluntary inspection of SCARDBs, Apex Weavers' Co-operative Societies and State Co-operative Marketing Federations. The frequency of statutory/voluntary inspections by NABARD was increased from 2005-06. The statutory inspections of CCBs and RRBs with positive net worth as also the voluntary inspections of Apex Co-operative Societies/Federations would continue to be conducted once in two years. With the introduction of annual inspections, the system of conducting quick inspections has been dispensed with.

The Board of Supervision (BoS) constituted by NABARD in 1999 to provide guidance and direction on matters relating to supervision of SCBs, CCBs and RRBs meets periodically and deliberates on such issues as listed below.

1. Review of insolvent SCBs and CCBs.
2. State-wise review of the functioning of co-operative credit institutions.
3. Review of off-site supervisory system (OSS).
4. Review of frauds, misappropriation, embezzlements, and defalcations.
5. Review of progress in implementation of the recommendations of the Advisory Committee on Flow of Credit to Agriculture and Related Activities (Chairman: V.S. Vyas).
6. Review of functioning of StCBs and SCARDBs based on inspection findings.
7. Procedure for receipt and follow-up of compliance reports on inspection findings.
8. Risk management systems in co-operative banks and RRBs.
9. Review of financial position of RRBs with deposit erosion of 25 percent or more.
10. Making applicable the revised prudential norms to SCARDBs and PCARDBs.

The Board has often expressed concern over: (a) deterioration in the financial position of many co-operative banks, (b) non-compliance by several banks with the provisions of Section 11(1) of the Banking Regulation Act, 1949 (AACS), relating to minimum capital requirement, and (c) absence of penal provision against the banks not adhering to the RBI's guidelines for asset classification and provisioning norms.

3.11 Problems of Rural Co-operatives

Rural co-operatives form an integral part of the rural credit system in India. They are the main source of institutional credit to the farmers. These societies are chiefly responsible for breaking the monopoly of moneylenders in providing credit to the agriculturists. There are around 1 lakh such societies in the country at present.

Despite the phenomenal outreach and volume of operations, the financial health of a very large proportion of rural credit co-operatives has deteriorated significantly. The institutions are beset with problems like low resource base, high dependence on external sources of funding, excessive governmental control, dual control, huge accumulated losses, imbalances, poor business diversification, low recovery etc. These institutions do not, therefore, inspire confidence among their existing and potential members, depositors, borrowers and lenders. Thus, there is a need to find ways for strengthening the co-operative movement and making it a well-managed and vibrant medium to serve the credit needs of rural India, especially the small and marginal farmers.

Moreover, these societies have paid inadequate attention to the needs of landless workers and rural artisans. Influential people in the villages have been the main beneficiaries of co-operative credit. Of late, there has been a tendency on the part of political leadership to write-off loans of the farmers. The RBI has repeatedly expressed concern in this regard because non-repayment of loans by the existing borrowers can adversely affect recycling of funds and the credit chances of the prospective borrowers. A national approach on this issue is required so that co-operative credit system may fulfil the task assigned to it.

It is part of a historic policy infirmity which allowed co-operatives to be treated as *refinance windows* instead of incentivising them into becoming genuine thrift and credit institutions.

The rural co-operative credit institutions are beset with many problems which include the following:

1. Low resource base.
2. High dependence on refinancing agencies.
3. Lack of diversification.
4. Huge accumulated losses.
5. Persistent non-performing assets (NPAs).
6. Low recovery levels.
7. Various other types of organisational weaknesses.

NABARD and the RBI, therefore, have been taking several supervisory and developmental measures in consultation with the Government of India for the revival of weak institutions and orderly growth of this important segment of the financial sector.

3.11.1 Problem of Triangular Regulation of Rural Co-operatives: In the case of the rural banking sector, apart from the presence of the Registrar of Co-operative Societies for incorporation/registration-related regulation, banking regulation is further split between the RBI, which has the regulatory powers, and NABARD which is vested with the supervisory responsibility. The shortcomings of this segregation of regulatory and supervisory roles is compounded by the fact that NABARD has limited powers of enforcement of its supervisory findings, for which it has to depend on either its own persuasiveness or seek action through interventions by the RBI or the State Government.

The *duality of control* over the co-operative institutions is a contentious issue. The Task Force on Co-operative Credit System (Chairman: Jagdish Capoor), 1999 addressed the issue of duality of control over co-operative credit institutions and suggested to remove the overlap of controls and endowing functional autonomy and operational freedom to co-operatives. The Task Force suggested to draw an Action Plan to redefine the roles and responsibilities and areas of regulation through delegation of powers in respect of all the players in the field, *viz.* the State Government, RBI, NABARD and co-operative institutions. In view of the weaknesses persisting in the co-operative banks, a system of preparation of institution-specific development action plans and execution of Memorandum of Understanding have been initiated since 2003- 04.

3.12 Task Force on Revival of Rural Co-operative Credit Institutions

The Government of India had constituted this Task Force (Chairman: A. Vaidyanathan), 2005 to propose an action plan for reviving the rural co-operative banking institutions and suggest an appropriate regulatory framework for these institutions. The Task Force in its Report submitted to the Central Government on February 15, 2005 made several recommendations to strengthen the rural co-operative credit structure in the country.

The major recommendations of the Task Force were as under:

- Co-operative credit structure (CCS) is impaired in governance, managerial and financial fronts and hence needs to be revived and restructured.
- Financial restructuring should be contingent on commitment to and implementation of legal and institutional reforms by the State Governments.
- Financial assistance should be made available for: (a) wiping out accumulated losses, (b) covering invoked but unpaid guarantees given by the State Governments, (c) increasing the capital to a specified minimum level, (d) retiring Government share capital, and (e) technical assistance.
- Availability of financial assistance from the Government

of India should be strictly subject to legal and institutional reforms in the co-operative sector to ensure that the co-operatives become truly democratic and member-driven. These reforms should include: (a) ensuring full voting membership rights on all users of financial services including depositors, (b) removing state intervention in administrative and financial matters in co-operatives, (c) removing provision for Government equity and participation in the Boards of Co-operatives, (d) withdrawing restrictive orders on financial matters, and (e) permitting co-operatives the freedom to take loans from any financial institution and not necessarily from only the upper tier and similarly place their deposits with any financial institution of their choice.

- The Task Force also recommended certain major amendments to the provisions of the Banking Regulation Act, 1949 enabling removal of dual control and bringing the co-operatives under the regulatory control of the RBI. These included: (a) all co-operative banks should be on par with the commercial banks as far as regulatory norms are concerned (b) RBI should prescribe *fit and proper* criteria for election to the Boards of Co-operative Banks, (c) RBI should prescribe certain criteria for professionals to be on the Boards of Co-operative Banks, (d) CEOs of the co-operative banks should be appointed by the respective banks themselves, and (e) co-operatives, other than co-operative banks as approved by the RBI, should not accept non-voting member deposits. Such co-operatives should also not use words such as *bank*, *banking*, *banker* or any other derivative of the word *bank* in their registered name.
- Total financial assistance was estimated tentatively at ₹ 14,839 crore. The Task Force, however, recommended a special audit to ascertain the exact requirement of assistance. The financial assistance should be shared by the Government of India, State Governments and the CCS, based on the origin of losses within a flexible matrix.

- NABARD should be designated as the nodal *implementing and pass through agency* to co-ordinate and monitor the progress of the programme representing the Government of India. NABARD should prepare model MoUs, model balance sheet proforma for PACS and CCBs.

3.13 Expert Group on Investment Credit in Agriculture, 2005

With a view to increasing the flow of credit to agriculture, the RBI set up this Expert Group (Chairman: Y.S.P. Thorat) to formulate a strategy for increasing investment credit in agriculture. The Group in its Report submitted in June 2005 identified several factors which constrain growth in investment in agriculture. These included the following.

- Meagre growth in minor irrigation and farm mechanization.
- Declining public sector investment.
- Limited credit absorptive capacity.
- Lack of effective mechanism for technology transfer and poor extension services.
- Inadequate extension services.
- Limited infrastructure for agro processing, storage, warehousing, value addition and marketing.
- Restrictions on purchases outside the *mandis.*
- Weather aberrations and output price fluctuations.
- Inadequate risk mitigation mechanism.
- Non-availability of land records.

The Group emphasised the need to accelerate investment in agriculture in order to achieve the desired level of growth. It also highlighted the need for investments to be appropriately structured, timed and well implemented in order to attain maximum effectiveness.

Major recommendations of the Group are set out below.

1. In view of various changes in the Indian rural canvas over the past few years, there is need for a shift in the thrust areas for investment credit to agriculture. Apart from the

traditional investments such as land development and irrigation, increased focus needs to be accorded to the entire supply chain management of agriculture products, reform of agriculture markets and public management in agricultural infrastructure.

2. State Governments need to lay emphasis on legal provisions/computerisation of land records, legal support for recovery, reforms in agricultural marketing, improving credit absorptive capacity through supporting infrastructure, strengthening infrastructure, improving extension network and developing marketing links.
3. NABARD should take special steps to facilitate capacity building of credit institutions in appraisal skill, particularly in North Eastern States, and design appropriate products for financing rural infrastructure projects outside the RIDF by mobilising resources from the market or banks at competitive rates of interest.
4. Water management policies and investment in water conservation be designed jointly by the State Governments and banks for improving productivity in agriculture.
5. The State Governments and NABARD should make investments in participatory community projects and in soil treatment to make wasteland and fallow land cultivable.
6. With a view to strengthening the institutional credit mechanism, short-term credit be integrated with term credit and efforts be made to reach the 'unreached' areas, promote supplementary credit delivery channels, outsource monitoring services, provide loan support for diversified agriculture, review HR policies, share the pool of technical expertise and make use of the model bankable projects prepared by NABARD.
7. The RBI along with banks could adopt agency models for credit delivery.
8. Government of India/State Governments and organisations engaged in agricultural research and development (R&D)

to reorient R&D activities.

9. To mitigate the risk in financing of agriculture, the Group suggested several measures. These included:

- developing suitable financial products and commodity exchanges;
- allowing banks to operate on behalf of farmers and participate in commodity futures;
- establishing a risk fund for fragile agriculture;
- designing special risk mitigation packages for low asset-based borrowers;
- using warehousing receipts with price hedging instruments;
- adopting technology for dissemination of market intelligence;
- sharing borrower information; and
- financing value chain by banks/through RIDF.

To sum up, though the network of commercial banks and RRBs has spread rapidly, their reach in the countryside both in terms of the number of clients and accessibility to the small and marginal farmers and other poorer segments is far less than that of co-operatives.

In spite of their suitability and useful role in building up a just socio-economic rural life, co-operative societies suffer from various weaknesses and their performance has been far from satisfactory in certain respects. The heavy overdues of co-operative societies are a cause for concern. The rising overdues have reduced the borrowing and lending activities of these societies. The increasing incidence of defaulting has brought bad name to these societies.

Co-operative societies have paid inadequate attention to the needs of landless workers and the rural artisans. The influential people in the villages have been the main beneficiaries of co-operative credit. Of late, there has been a tendency on the part of political leadership to write off the loans of the farmers. The RBI has repeatedly expressed concern in this regard because the non-repayment of loans by the existing borrowers adversely affects recycling of funds and the credit chances of prospective borrowers. A national approach on this issue is required so that co-operative credit system may fulfil the task assigned to it.

Positive impact of reforms, as has been witnessed in the case of commercial banking sector, may take longer to get manifested for co-operative banks given the late start of the reform process in this sector. Unless such a positive scenario evolves for the co-operative banking sector in the near future, the financial health of many of these banks would continue to remain a cause of concern.

It is imperative that the government takes initiatives to expand the network of institutional credit facilities in the rural areas and that the credit needs of the small and marginal farmers are met through earmarking credit for the group. Extension and marketing initiatives need to focus on this segment. At the same time, group initiatives need to be encouraged and awareness among the group has to be increased. The procedural formalities also have to be made less stringent to make the system more user-friendly for the largely illiterate group.

4

Urban Co-operative Banks (UCBs) in India

The financial sector reforms have been important components of the overall economic reforms undertaken in India since 1991. Financial reforms have also envisaged improving the efficiency and productivity of the co-operative credit delivery system which, in turn, would accelerate the requisite credit flow to the productive sectors of the economy.

The major objectives of these reforms in the co-operative sector have been as under:

1. To make the institutions competitive by removing external constraints having a bearing on their operations.
2. To improve their financial health.
3. To ensure transparency in their business operations.
4. To improve their profitability.
5. Institutional building and strengthening.

Positive impact of reforms, as has been witnessed in the case of commercial banking sector, may take longer to get manifested for co-operative banks given the late start of the reform process in this sector. Unless such a positive scenario evolves for the co-operative banking sector in the near future, the financial health of many of these banks would continue to remain a cause of concern.

4.1 Role of UCBs

The co-operative banking system forms an integral part of the Indian financial system. It comprises urban co-operative banks and rural co-operative credit institutions. Urban co-operative banks have a single-tier structure whereas rural co-operatives have a two- or three-tier structure.

The single tier urban co-operative banks (UCBs)—also

referred to as primary co-operative banks—play an important role in meeting the growing credit needs of urban and semi-urban areas of the country. The UCBs, which grew rapidly in the early 1990s, showed certain weaknesses arising out of lack of sound corporate governance, unethical lending, comparatively high levels of non-performing loans and their inability to operate in a liberalised environment. Accordingly, some of the weak UCBs have been either liquidated or merged with other banks.

Co-operative banks in India are more than 100 years old. These banks came into existence with the enactment of the Agricultural Credit Co-operative Societies Act in 1904. Co-operative banks form an integral part of the banking system in India. These banks operate mainly for the benefit of rural areas, particularly the agricultural sector. Co-operative banks mobilise deposits and supply agricultural and rural credit with a wider outreach. They are the main source of institutional credit to the farmers. Co-operative banks are chiefly responsible for breaking the monopoly of moneylenders in providing credit to agriculturists. They have also been an important instrument for various development schemes, particularly subsidy-based programmes for the poor. Co-operative banks operate for non-agricultural sector also but their role is small.

Though much smaller as compared to scheduled commercial banks, co-operative banks constitute an important segment of the Indian banking system. They have an extensive branch network and reach out to people in remote areas. They have traditionally played an important role in creating banking habits among the lower and middle-income groups and in strengthening the rural credit delivery system.

Urban co-operative banks play an important role in meeting the growing credit needs of urban and semi-urban areas. UCBs mobilise savings from the middle and lower income groups and purvey credit to small borrowers, including weaker sections of the society. Scheduled UCBs are under closer regulatory and supervisory framework of the RBI.

The financial reforms process initiated in 1991 has tried to achieve regulatory convergence among various financial intermediaries in view of their systemic importance. Therefore, the basic objectives and instruments of reforms for co-operative banks have been the same as for State Co-operative Banks (SCBs). However, given the special characteristics of co-operative banks, they have been extended certain dispensations in terms of pace and sequencing of reforms.

UCBs have grown rapidly since the early 1990s. During the phase of rapid expansion, however, the sector showed certain weaknesses arising out of: (a) lack of sound corporate governance, (b) unethical lending, (c) comparatively high level of loan defaults, and (d) inability to operate in a liberalised and competitive environment. The RBI, therefore, has been striving to harness the growth of UCBs with appropriate application of prudential regulation and supervision to safeguard the interests of depositors.

Keeping in view the weak financial position of many UCBs, the RBI has undertaken a series of measures directed towards strengthening of the UCBs. Since March 31, 1993, the UCBs have been advised to adhere to the prudential norms which include, *inter alia*, the following.

1. Applying capital adequacy standards.
2. Prescribing an asset-liability management framework.
3. Enhancing the proportion of holding of Government and other approved securities for the purpose of statutory liquidity ratio (SLR) stipulation.
4. Restriction on bank finance against the security of corporate shares and debentures.
5. Limiting the exposure to capital market investment.

In view of the challenges arising from the functioning of the UCBs for the financial system, the RBI appointed a High Power Committee (Chairman: K. Madhava Rao), 1999 to review the performance of UCBs and to suggest necessary measures to strengthen this sector. Based on the recommendations of this Committee, measures have been initiated to strengthen the existing urban banking structure.

4.2 Relaxation of Investment Portfolios of UCBs

UCBs were given some relaxation in the prudential norms for their investment portfolio in September 2004. They were allowed to exceed the limit of 25 percent of total investment under held till maturity (HTM) category provided: (a) the excess comprises only SLR securities, and (b) total SLR securities held in HTM category are not more than 25 percent of their net demand and time liabilities (NDTL) as on the last Friday of the second preceding fortnight.

Taking into account the difficulties faced by UCBs in meeting the provisioning requirements, it was further decided, as a special case, to consider relaxing the provisioning requirements both for scheduled UCBs and non-scheduled UCBs. Accordingly, scheduled UCBs were advised that they may crystallise the provisioning requirement arising on account of shifting of securities from HFT/AFS categories to HTM category consequent to the issue of guidelines dated September 2, 2004 and amortise the same over a maximum period of five years commencing from the accounting year ended March 31, 2005, with a minimum of 20 percent of such amount each year.

As regards non-scheduled UCBs, they were allowed to shift securities from HFT/AFS categories to HTM category at book value, subject to the following conditions. First, in case the book value is higher than the face value, the difference between the book value and the face value, i.e. the premium may be amortised in equal instalment over the remaining period to maturity. If the security was obtained at a discount to face value, the difference should be booked as profit only at the time of maturity of the security.

Second, the securities transferred under this special dispensation should be kept separately under HTM category and should not be transferred back to the HFT/AFS category in future in terms of the existing instruction of transfer of securities from HTM category. Third, in normal course, such securities under HTM category should not be sold in the market and redeemed on maturity only. However, in exceptional circumstances, if such securities are to be sold, profit on sale of investments in this category should be first taken to the *profit and loss account* and thereafter be appropriated to the *capital reserve*. Loss on sale will be recognised in the *profit and loss account* in the year of sale.

4.3 Restructuring of UCBs with Negative Net Worth

A policy regarding restructuring of scheduled UCBs with negative net worth has also been formulated by the RBI. The RBI has begun a consultative process with a few scheduled UCBs with negative net worth by involving officials of the concerned State Governments and banks with a view to revitalising and rehabilitating them. The emphasis is on a time-bound programme by identifying the contours of their rehabilitation plan and setting up monitorable milestones. The RBI will be closely monitoring the achievements of the banks *vis-à-vis* the targets set at regular intervals and initiate appropriate action with a view to protecting depositors' interest and avoiding systemic problems. Issues relating to large depositors, part conversion of deposits into equity, reduction of non-performing assets, human resources and technological development and the support from the State Governments would be examined.

The option of merger/amalgamation could also be explored, wherever necessary. The RBI would limit its examinations and approvals to the banking and regulatory issues to satisfy itself that the restructuring package is in the interests of the depositors and the public at large. The RBI would also take into account various other parameters such as infusion of funds, sacrifice by stake holders, restructuring of liabilities, recovery of NPAs, regulatory support and forbearance, governance, business plan, and filing of applications and documents.

4.4 Regulation and Supervision of UCBs

The regulation and supervision of the urban co-operative banks (UCBs) was brought within the ambit of the RBI's statutory control under the Banking Laws (as Applicable to Co-operative Societies) Act, which came into force from March 1, 1966. The regulatory powers conferred on the RBI with regard to co-operative banks are limited. While the principles of supervision with regard to co-operative banks have been formulated and implemented by the RBI in respect of UCBs under the Banking Regulation Act, 1949, the Act does not apply to primary agricultural credit societies and land development banks, thus leaving them under the regulatory purview of the State.

Instances such as the Madhavapura Mercantile Co-operative Bank's failure brought to the fore the need to have stringent regulatory control over the co-operative banking system. In order to strengthen the supervisory mechanism, the RBI extended the Off-site Surveillance System (OSS) to all non-scheduled UCBs having deposit size of ₹ 100 crore and above. A supervisory reporting system was introduced for the scheduled UCBs from March 2001 as a first step towards setting up of OSS for all UCBs. The capital adequacy norms were introduced in a phased manner from March 2002. Better risk management through avoidance of concentration of credit risk, off-site surveillance for non-schedule UCBs and following up of Know Your Customer (KYC) guidelines have also been introduced to strengthen the UCBs.

A total ban has been imposed since October 2003 on grant of loans and advances to directors of UCBs, their relatives and concerns in which they have interest with a view to preventing certain irregularities. The RBI has also directed that UCBs should undertake usual due diligence in respect of investments in non-SLR securities. The RBI introduced a new system of grading of UCBs in April 2003, which is based on their

CRAR, level of net NPAs, record of losses and compliance with regulatory environment. Similarly, a system of supervisory rating for UCBs under the CAMELS model has also been introduced. Initially, it was implemented for scheduled UCBs but subsequently its simplified version was extended to non-scheduled UCBs in March 2004.

Despite the structural and cultural differences between UCBs and commercial banks, the above measures suggest that the RBI has been exercising its regulatory and supervisory powers to ensure that the co-operative credit structure is strengthened on the lines similar to the regulation and supervision of commercial banks.

The RBI is entrusted with the responsibility of regulation and supervision of the banking-related activities of UCBs under the Banking Regulation Act, 1949 As Applicable to Co-operative Societies (AACS). Other aspects such as incorporation, registration, administration, management and winding-up of UCBs are supervised and regulated by the respective State Governments through Registrars of Co-operative Societies (RCS) under the Co-operative Societies Acts of the respective States. UCBs with a multi-state presence are registered under the Multi-State Co-operative Societies Act, 2002 and are regulated and supervised jointly by the Central Government through Central Registrar of Co-operative Societies and the RBI.

Thus, current legislative framework provides for dual control over UCBs. For resolving problems arising out of dual control regime, a draft legislative bill proposing certain amendments to the Banking Regulation Act, 1949, based on the recommendations of the High Powered Committee on UCBs, was forwarded to the Government. Pending the amendment to the Act, the RBI is entering into a regulatory arrangement with the State Governments through Memorandum of Understanding (MoU) to facilitate proper and coordinated regulation and supervision of UCBs. MoUs have already been signed between the RBI and three States that have a large network of UCBs, *viz.* Andhra Pradesh, Gujarat and Karnataka. As a follow-up to the signing of MoUs, the RBI has constituted State Level Task Force for Urban Co-operative Banks (TAFCUBs) in these States.

4.5 Mergers/Amalgamations of UCBs

With a view to encouraging and facilitating consolidation and emergence of strong entities and as well as for providing an avenue for non-disruptive exit of weak/unviable entities in the co-operative banking sector, guidelines were issued to facilitate merger/amalgamation in the sector. The RBI, while considering proposals for merger/amalgamation, confines its approval to the financial aspects of the merger taking into consideration the interests of depositors and financial stability. The RBI considers proposals subject to the post-merger entity meeting the prescribed following prudential norms.

1. When the net worth of the acquired bank is positive and the acquirer bank assures to protect entire deposits of all the depositors of the acquired bank.
2. When the net worth of acquired bank is negative but the acquirer bank, on its own, assures to protect deposits of all the depositors of the acquired bank.
3. When the net worth of the acquired bank is negative and the acquirer bank assures to protect the deposits of all the depositors with financial support from the State Government extended upfront as part of the process of merger.

4.6 Problem of Dual Control in Co-operative Banking

The single most important regulatory and supervisory weakness that persists in the co-operative banking sector is the prevalence of dual control. While incorporation/registration and management-related activities are regulated in the states by the Registrar of Co-operative Societies or the Central Registrar of Co-operative Societies (for multi-state co-operative banks), banking-related activities are under the regulatory/supervisory purview of the Reserve Bank of India

(RBI) or NABARD. The basic issue is that co-operation is a state subject under the Indian Constitution and as such *co-operatives* as a form of organisation are governed by the State Co-operative Societies Act, irrespective of whether they are banks or other forms of co-operative entities.

This duality of control and the absence of a clear demarcation of functions between the regulators have engaged the attention of a number of committees in the past. While in the case of commercial banks the RBI has the powers under the Banking Regulation Act, 1949 to deal with crucial aspects of functioning such as supersession of the board of directors, appointment of liquidators, initiating action for removal of the CEO/Chairman of a bank, instituting special audits, and conducting statutory audit through external chartered accountants. In the case of co-operative banks these powers are subordinated in a way by the requirement that all such actions would require the intervention/approval of the Registrar of Co-operative Societies of the respective State Governments or the Central Registrar of Co-operative Societies, as the case may be.

This duality of control affects the quality of supervision and regulation, and it also affects the functioning of co-operative banks. The regulatory weaknesses foster inefficiency and impede the development of governance principles. Moreover, it burdens the banks with multiple levels of compliance and reporting requirements.

4.7 Impairment in Governance and Management

A unique feature of the co-operative banking system in India is that borrowers have a significant say in the management of the bank. This follows from the fact that only borrowers of the co-operative bank are eligible to be its members, contributing to share capital. As the Board Members of the bank are elected by borrowers, it results in the policies of the bank not always being in congruence with the interests of depositors. In view of the propensity of these banks to pursue borrower-oriented policies rather than policies that should be in favour of protecting interest of depositors, it has often been suggested that the involvement of depositors in the management of these banks should be enhanced by encouraging membership of depositors on par with borrowers.

Another reason for impairment of governance in the co-operative banking structure is attributed to interference in matters related to appointment of directors on the basis of political affiliations rather than on merit. This manifests itself in lack of professional expertise at the board level and interference in decision-making, particularly in respect of loan sanctions. This impairs the financial health of co-operative banks.

4.8 Working Group on IT Support for UCBs

In today's financial systems, usage of Information Technology is fundamental to the survival and growth of the institutions. IT usage not only help banks hold and reduce their cost of operations, several developments in the information and communication technology (ICT) enable the institutions to offer highly profitable products and services to their constituents. IT has become not just an enabler, but also the distinguishing and differentiator; it also provides competitive advantage and edge to its user. Further, current regulatory and supervisory compliance demands that the institutions have a very sound usage of IT systems for their operations.

The Vision Document for urban co-operative banks (UCBs), released in March 2005, proposed signing of memorandum of understanding (MoU) between RBI and Central and respective State governments for establishing a consultative approach to supervision and regulation of UCBs. The Reserve Bank has so far signed such MoUs with 16 State Governments and the Central Government.

In terms of the MoUs, the RBI is committed to facilitate IT initiatives in UCBs. In furtherance of the commitment made under the MoUs, Governor announced in the Mid-term Review of the Annual Policy 2007-08, that 'a working group comprising representatives of the Reserve Bank, State Governments and the UCBs sector' would be constituted 'to examine the various areas where IT support could be provided by the Reserve Bank.' Accordingly, the RBI constituted a Working Group on IT Support for Urban Co-operative Banks (Chairman: R. Gandhi) on December 19, 2007 with the following Terms of Reference:

1. To review the current level and use of IT infrastructure in UCBs.
2. To structure a model/benchmark level of IT infrastructure for UCBs in general or for identified sub groups of UCBs.
3. To prepare a suggested roadmap of building such an infrastructure by the UCBs.
4. To identify areas and ways in which IT support may be provided by the RBI.
5. To make recommendations on the nature, scope and delivery mechanism for IT support to UCBs by the RBI.

4.8.1 Findings of the Working Group: There exists a wide disparity with regard to the usage of Information Technology by the Urban Co-operative Banks. As on March 31, 2007, 16 out of 1853 banks had implemented Core Banking Solutions, while about 50 banks did not even have computers. The remaining banks exist somewhere along the continuum between those that had CBS on the one hand, and those without even PCs on the other.

Most banks have solutions based on Total Branch Automation. Several banks have implemented locally developed and customised application solutions. While some big UCBs have in-house IT wings to take care of development and maintenance of systems, most banks have outsourced these services.

Anecdotal evidences are there about the problems faced by these banks because of their small size, lack of adequate IT knowledge, lack of adequate IT savvy manpower and small time vendors. They had suffered because small vendors could not provide satisfactory AMC and adequate post-implementation support for making changes in the software on account of their inability to retain skilled staff or sometimes because of the small scale of their operations, which rendered them unviable. Moreover, such legacy systems, set up by small vendors, were not standardized and therefore made migration to new systems more cumbersome and expensive than even acquiring a new one.

The acquisition of non-standardized software/software developed by local/regional level vendors is fraught with the following risks:

1. **Vendor Disappearance:** Vendors who developed software for small banks are often small-time operators and are not available for support, modifications and change management subsequently. Their mortality rate is often high. Eventually, the software became obsolete and redundant.
2. **Loss of Key Personnel by Vendor:** Some times, the vendor is available but the key personnel, who were involved in the development of software, are no more with the vendor. The vendor finds it difficult to extend the required level of the support without its skilled personnel as being small it has little flexibility in the absence of backup staff. As they often also do not follow standard practice of software development and documentation, the maintenance and updation of source-codes becomes difficult for the new personnel.
3. **Lack of Regulatory Compliance Modules:** Almost all the small-vendor developed software systems do not contain important regulatory provisions such as compliance to KYC norms, etc.

The Group also observed that there were several large banks which had their own data centres and were offering core banking solutions to the smaller banks and that a few successful cases of sharing of data centre facilities among banks were also known. However, as awareness of IT among UCBs was not pervasive, several banks seemed reluctant to keep their data in the data centres owned by other bank/banks.

4.8.2 Problem Analysis and Possible Solutions: Considering the increasing penetration of commercial banks in what till recently were the niche areas of UCBs (such as middle and low income housing finance/retail loans etc.), the need to computerize the operations of even the smallest UCBs has become imperative to improve customer service and ensure survival. While deliberating upon the level of computerization of UCBs, the Group noted that in a country like China, all the two-lakh odd branches of all the banks had been computerized.

The Group, while noting with satisfaction that the front line UCBs have taken advantage of what the ICT can offer, also observed that a very large proportion of UCBs have not done the same. Among UCBs, considering the high concentration of very small banks, lack of uniformity in the levels of computerization and inadequate awareness about effectiveness of computers in enhancing competitiveness, the Group felt that it is necessary to articulate the minimum IT infrastructure which should exist in each UCB regardless of its size, location or profitability.

This minimum level of IT infrastructure, the Group felt should include the following:

1. Computerized front-end i.e. customer interface;
2. Automatic backend accounting (through software);
3. Computerized MIS reporting; and
4. Automated regulatory reporting.

The above minimum benchmark for computerization does not include 'networking' among branches, since the sector is largely dominated by unit banks or banks with only a few branches.

The Group then discussed about various methods by which a bank can create IT infrastructure for its use. In view of the variance in size, financial strength and IT capabilities of UCBs, the Group also considered the possibility of sharing of IT infrastructure at the state level as state was operationally a logical unit for UCBs which are under the regulation of state governments and RBI.

While an arms' length distance between banks owning the data centre and the database of other UCBs using the facility is technologically feasible, it also needs to be recognized that the long-term sustainability of such an arrangement is an issue, as banks are essentially in the business of banking and activities like development and maintenance of data centres and providing software support to financial institutions are focussed functions of IT firms.

4.8.3 Recommendations: Usage of Information Technology for financial systems in the modern world is fundamental to the survival and growth of the institutions. IT usage not only helps banks hold and reduce their cost of operations, several developments in the information and communication technology (ICT) enable the institutions to proffer highly profitable products and services to their constituents. IT has become not just an enabler, but also the distinguishing factor and differentiator. It also provides competitive advantage and edge to its users. Further, current regulatory and supervisory compliance demands that the institutions have a very sound usage of IT systems for their operations.

A. Minimum Information Technology Infrastructure in UCBs: Considering the concentration of small UCBs, the lack of uniformity in the levels of computerization and inadequate awareness about the efficacy of computers in enhancing competitiveness, the Group felt it necessary to articulate the minimum IT infrastructure which should exist in each UCB regardless of its size, location or profitability. This minimum level of IT infrastructure should include the following:

1. Computerized front-end i.e. customer interface.
2. Automatic backend accounting (through software).
3. Computerized MIS reporting.
4. Automated regulatory reporting.

B. UCBs to be Supported: While maximum support is

required for the small/weak banks, if support is extended only to the weak or small banks, the better performing or growing banks may tend to interpret that they were indirectly suffering because of their good performance or growth as RBI was not extending support to them for their IT efforts. As such, the group felt that support should be structured in such a way that it can be offered to all.

C. Nature of Support: In order to implement the minimum level of IT infrastructure by the UCBs as indicated in Recommendation No. 1, core banking solution (CBS) would be required to be adopted by the banks. The model of CBS may be according to the size and spread of the banks.

The models for acquiring the IT infrastructure could be one of the following:

(a) Application Service Provider (ASP) Model: In respect of the small banks, particularly the unit banks, it was felt that the best method for computerization could be through the ASP model as the problems of software development and maintenance, training and retention of IT professionals, installation and maintenance of complex and costly hardware and other logistics like data centres etc would be addressed by the service provider without need for much initiative or involvement of the UCB. An agency like IDRBT could short-list/select one/few vendors and be the conduit and service quality assuror to the banks. The payment model for the ASP option includes a one time payment and a small charge every month combined with per transaction fee, which could also be suitable for the smaller banks. Moreover, in ASP model, initial investment would be less and by combining the requirements of a large number of banks the cost could be further reduced.

(b) Outright Purchase Model: If banks seek to go for outright purchase of the Core Banking, including data centre, the cost would be in the range of ₹ 1.5 crore to ₹ 2 crore for 5-10 branches per bank. Further, availability and retention of IT savvy professionals are also to be ensured. Besides, the bank should be strong enough to enforce service quality by the vendor. The Group feels that only those banks which are well capitalised and with good track record, on whom we have confidence and comfort that the end use of funds are assured, and that they have IT savvy personnel to implement/oversee and deal with the vendors and for whom investing in an outright purchase option is financially a preferable option should be given the option to choose this model. As such, banks which have a business of more than ₹ 100 crore, CRAR of over 9 percent and have been profit making for the past 3 years could be provided support for outright purchase.

(c) Delivery Mechanism: As indicated above, the support will be available for all UCBs. However, it should not be given in the form of a grant; support may be in the form of a loan and not subsidy.

Experience shows that subsidy tends to reduce seriousness regarding the end use of funds. Financial support may be extended as follows:

1. Support could be in the form of interest free loan, repayable in 7 years, with one year moratorium. UCBs would be eligible for loan for software as also for purchase of hardware.
2. In the case of big banks preferring to go for outright purchase of software and hardware, interest free with only service charge of ½ percent to 1 percent to be charged by the SCB routing the loan may be considered.
3. In respect of weak/sick banks, the 'moratorium' may be for two years. In case the UCB defaults on its repayment obligations even after that, a view may be taken at that point regarding other options like continuation of management, non-disruptive exit of the bank etc.
4. For the banks which have to adopt ASP Model, routing of the interest-free loan by the Reserve Bank could be through IDRBT, which could prepare Systems Requirement Specifications, select vendors, prepare development/testing and implementation plans, and vetting the SLA (Service Level Agreement) between users i.e. UCBs and the service

providing entity, to ensure smooth implementation and post-implementation support by the vendor.

5. For the banks which elect to have outright purchase of the application system, the Group felt that the Reserve Bank may not be able to extend direct loans due to monetary policy implications. However, NABARD has a separate fund for IT usage in co-operative sector, a portion of which can be routed to UCBs, through SCCB/DCCBs.
6. If required, IDRBT may develop an area of expertise within itself to cater to the IT needs of small banks, including UCBs. National and State Federation of co-operatives may also think of creating such IT facilities for UCBs in the long run for the benefit of the sector.

(d) Conditionality:

1. The aforementioned facilities will be made available only for UCBs located in the MOU states.
2. Even if the UCB is a loss-making one, it would still have to honour repayment obligations in respect of the interest-free loan/loan from NABARD.
3. In case any UCB needs customization/change in the package for particular functionalities, it may put in a request to IDRBT, which will make arrangements for the same. However, such changes/enhancements will have to be paid for by the concerned UCB.
4. In case of banks which already have software in their existing branches, interest-free loan would be available for meeting cost of upgradation and/or expansion, under the same terms and conditions.
5. A bonus could be considered for the banks which repay the instalments on time and/or earlier. The bonus could be in the form of waiving the last instalment.

4.9 Working Group on Umbrella Organization and Revival Fund for Urban Co-operative Banks

There are a large number of primary (urban) co-operative banks (UCBs) in the country forming a heterogeneous group in terms of size and spread. Many of these banks are very small in size and reach. They compete with larger participants in the same banking space. Over the years, a number of UCBs have become weak and non-viable thus posing systemic risk to the UCB sector. They lack avenues for raising capital funds since they cannot go in for public issue of shares nor can they issue shares to members at a premium. At the same time, there are a number of UCBs in the sector that are financially strong and viable. Some sort of co-operative bonding and mutual support system could make the sector strong and vibrant. Looking at various successful federal models internationally, especially in Europe and USA, a need was felt for an umbrella organization that would be in a position to channelize their resources, aggregate their needs and also lend credibility through mutual support in the financial market.

In this backdrop, it was decided by the RBI to constitute a Working Group (Chairman: V.S. Das) on May 28, 2008 to suggest measures including the appropriate regulatory and supervisory framework, to facilitate emergence of umbrella organization(s) for the UCB sector in the respective states. Further, the Standing Advisory Committee for UCBs has opined that the Working Group may also look into the issues concerning creation of Revival Fund for the sector.

4.9.1 Terms of Reference of the Working Group:

1. To study the regulatory and supervisory structure of umbrella organizations of financial co-operative institutions/banks, as prevalent in other parts of the world, especially in relation to raising of capital and intra co-operative group support system.
2. To study the existing structure and legal framework for UCBs in India and to examine the need and scope for a federated structure/umbrella organization for UCBs at the state level.
3. To suggest appropriate supervisory and regulatory framework to facilitate emergence of such umbrella organisation(s) for UCBs, taking into consideration the

international experiences and systems.

4. To study and suggest modalities for setting up an appropriate mutual assistance/revival fund for urban co-operative banks and the nature of support that could be provided by such fund.

4.9.2 Recommendations:

A. Need for Umbrella Organization: Urban Co-operative Banks in India cater to the financial needs of the middle and lower middle class people in metropolitan, urban and semi-urban centres. They operate on a standalone basis, unlike rural co-operatives in India, which have a three tier structure. These banks are large in number, though of varied asset size, ranging from small to medium. Although they compete with commercial banks, their share in total deposits is barely 4 percent. There is a significant part of the UCB sector that lacks professionalism and is unable to keep pace with rapid advancements in IT, modern banking systems and financial products. The sector also has significant number of banks which are weak and need financial support. There have been occasions when, due to contagion effect, banks have encountered liquidity problems. Being in the nature of co-operative societies, the UCBs' ability to augment their capital is also restricted, thereby hindering their growth.

The organizational structure of UCBs, their small size and limited area of operation add to their vulnerability. Further, in the wake of advances in information and communication technology, payment and settlement systems and services, they need to widen their range of services to run on professional lines and match the services provided by commercial banks.

Internationally, co-operative banks, popularly called Credit Unions, operate in networks and have an entity which provides a wide range of services to them, such as, fund management services, lines of credit, asset management, payment and settlement system gateway, ATM networks, credit card, investment, securitisation, capital raising and other financial services. These entities act as Umbrella Organizations and the networks provide co-operative solidarity. International experience has shown that the presence of such an Umbrella Organization has contributed towards the member credit unions being stable, sound and efficient entities.

B. Umbrella Organization at the National Level: The Working Group carefully went into the important issue of whether in India we should have an Umbrella Organization at the national level or whether each state should have its own Umbrella Organization. While countries such as Canada and USA have provincial Umbrella Organizations, Australia and European countries have preferred to consolidate and have national level organizations.

UCBs in India are not evenly spread across the country. They have predominant presence in five states, viz. Andhra Pradesh, Gujarat, Karnataka, Maharashtra and Tamil Nadu accounting for about 89 percent of the total business of the sector. Further, UCBs in Maharashtra alone had about 64 percent of the total business. In contrast, their presence was minimal in many states. Considering the regional spread and market share of UCBs, the Working Group is of the opinion that having multiple umbrella organizations for UCBs in India or state-wise umbrellas may be neither feasible nor desirable. Therefore, the Working Group is of the view that there should be one Umbrella Organization at the national level for the entire UCB sector.

C. Functions of the Umbrella Organization: The Umbrella Organization should act as a central credit institution for UCBs, like similar organizations abroad for Credit Unions. It should provide a wide range of services such as providing loans and advances, refinance, payment and settlement services, IT services, ATM network services, investment banking, fund management, management consultancy, capacity building services and even capital support. The UCB sector was found to be particularly keen that the organization provides payment and settlement services and liquidity assistance. This may possibly be emanating from the concern arising in the context of implementation of the new eligibility norms for MICR clearing, RTGS, SGL/CSGL accounts and making them out of reach for a large number of UCBs and lack of avenues for temporary liquidity assistance (even against SLR securities) in case of need and urgency; more so in case of run like situations. Similarly, many small UCBs are looking forward to a centralized agency for buying, selling and managing Government securities on their behalf in view of their lack of skill and expertise in the areas. The Working Group recommends that the Umbrella Organization should provide a whole range of services to member UCBs, as described above.

D. Form of Organization of the Umbrella Organization: The Working Group observed that non-banking financial companies (NBFCs) could perform most of the functions of Umbrella Organization. The minimum start-up capital for such companies has been stipulated at ₹ 2 crore, for the present, as per the Reserve Bank's policy for issue of certification for registration. The Working Group is of the view that even though contribution to share capital of the Umbrella Organization would be voluntary, the initial start-up capital could easily be garnered from UCBs.

It would be better to build the edifice, brick by brick, with low start-up capital and augment the capital funds over the years, rather than to commit huge capital funds from the co-operative sector, which itself is facing difficulties in raising capital.

Further, at present, the Reserve Bank has been vested with adequate power to regulate and supervise NBFCs. The current RBI regulations, however, do not permit NBFC to undertake certain activities and place restrictions on certain others; more importantly, the Payment and Settlement services.

Considering that access to payment and settlement gateways and dealing platforms for securities through Umbrella Organization are the most sought after services, the Working Group was of the view that it would be within the powers of the Reserve Bank to grant regulatory permissions/ forbearances wherever necessary, depending upon the type of functions. NBFCs may be broadly divided into deposit taking and non-deposit taking. The term "deposit", however, does not include amount of money received from banks and financial institutions and further, the term "public deposit" excludes certain categories of deposits. The NBFCs that are authorized to accept/hold public deposits need to have minimum net owned funds and they are required to maintain certain specified percentage (15 percent) of the public deposits in liquid assets in the form of approved securities and unencumbered term deposits with scheduled commercial banks.

These NBFCs should achieve minimum investment grade credit rating for accepting public deposits. The regulations for the deposit taking NBFCs are tighter than that of non-deposit taking. On the contrary, a non-deposit taking NBFC enjoys more freedom in undertaking its business, more particularly deployment of its funds. Keeping in view the extant regulations applicable and the relative merits of deposit taking and non-deposit taking NBFCs, the Working Group is of the opinion that to start with, a non-deposit taking NBFC may be the most suitable form of organization and recommends that Umbrella Organization may be initially set up as a non-deposit taking NBFC. The Umbrella Organization in the form of a non-deposit taking NBFC would, however, access money from UCBs and others, which are not treated as public deposits. The conversion of the Umbrella Organization to a banking company could be considered in due course in the light of experience gained.

E. Authorized Capital, Subscribed/Paid up Capital: The Working Group deliberated at length on the modus operandi of raising share capital for the Umbrella Organization. It was felt that share capital of the Umbrella Organization should be closely held by the UCBs and subscription should be voluntary. However, some members strongly felt that contribution to the share capital of the Umbrella Organization should be made compulsory for UCBs and the Reserve Bank could consider issuing direction to UCBs in this regard. The Group discussed the pros and cons of the proposal and was of the view that though equity participation by all UCBs should be encouraged; there could be constraints to make it compulsory for UCBs. The Group was of the view that both the options should be kept open. The National and State Federations should educate UCBs about the benefits of having an Umbrella Organization and also play a big role for its set up and raising of capital.

F. Sources of Working Capital: To begin with, the capital funds would normally go to finance fixed assets of Umbrella Organization and the balance amount could be used for financing activities. Umbrella Organization would also need some source of working capital. Being a non-deposit taking NBFC, it would have access to the following sources for its working capital:

1. Borrowings from banks/financial institutions.
2. Deposits: term deposits from UCBs.
3. Debt instruments: bonds/debentures.
4. Refinance: against financial assets (loans and advances) including securities.
5. Other miscellaneous sources.

The Umbrella Organization would need to have access to deposits from UCBs, which could be a major source of working capital for carrying out its business. A significant number of UCBs have low credit deposit ratios and they park their surplus funds with DCCB/SCB and commercial banks. Umbrella Organization, being the central credit institution for UCBs, may be able to tap these deposits for its financing and investment activities.

G. CRR and SLR: The Working Group feels that it would be attractive for UCBs to place deposits with Umbrella Organization if these deposits are treated as CRR/SLR. The Umbrella Organization would definitely need such deposits to meet its working capital requirements. The Working Group, therefore, recommends that the Reserve Bank may consider exempting UCBs placing term deposits with the Umbrella Organization from maintenance of SLR in the form of Government and other approved securities up to 15 percent of their NDTL. The Working Group also feels that this would serve as an incentive for UCBs to take up membership of the Umbrella Organization. The Working Group feels that the Reserve Bank which has been instrumental in promoting several developmental and financial institutions should consider the recommendation positively and favourably as the Umbrella Organization is being conceptualized to provide the much needed stability to the UCB sector that would also contribute to financial stability.

H. Business Profile and Sources of Income: Profitability of the UO's operations is very crucial and, therefore, in most countries, the central credit institutions have a significant asset portfolio outside the captive business. Further, its ability to raise capital and debt in the market would also depend upon the strength of its balance sheet. The Working Group, therefore, recommends that UO should delicately balance its commitment towards UCB sector and the need to keep its asset portfolio strong and healthy.

As the Umbrella Organization would function as a central credit institution, it would orient its business to provide various services to the member UCBs (loans and advances, refinance, payment and settlement services, IT services, ATM network services, investment banking, fund management and capital support). This would fetch it revenue in the form of interest, commission, exchange, etc. It is felt that the income derived from services extended to the UCB sector may not be sufficient to sustain the Umbrella Organization. The large and strong UCBs may not avail some of the services. However, small and medium sized UCBs are expected to avail most services for their clients and for themselves, as they may not be eligible for carrying out such activities on their own. The

Umbrella Organization's asset portfolio would predominantly comprise loans and advances, which would involve more than the normal risk as many of the UCBs are small entities and have local operations. The Umbrella Organization could also lend to non-UCBs. It would also need to have a healthy investment portfolio.

I. Management: It goes without saying that an Umbrella Organization, such as the one under design should be run on thoroughly professional lines and observe the best practices insofar as corporate governance is concerned. The Working Group recommends that the Memorandum and Articles of Association of the company (Umbrella Organization) should specifically provide for appointment of independent directors. In order to achieve this objective, the fit and proper criteria for the Board of Directors and Executive Board/CEO may be prescribed either in the Memorandum and Articles of Association, or by the regulators.

CEO should be a professional of repute, with deep knowledge and understanding of the UCB sector, combined with business acumen of a finance company to inspire confidence in the Umbrella Organization. The Working Group leaves it to the Reserve Bank for putting in place a suitable system, standards and stringent fit and proper criteria to ensure that the position of CEO is held by a competent person. The Working Group is also of the considered view that the Reserve Bank should nominate on the Board a suitable officer, at least during the initial formative years of the Umbrella Organization. Subsequently, the Reserve Bank may have an Observer on the Board. This would not only lend the Umbrella Organization greater credibility, but its nominee's guidance would also be useful in adherence to best corporate governance practices, regulations and formulation of appropriate business strategies and products.

J. Emergency Liquidity and Solvency Support: Occasionally, UCBs confronted by financial distress, caused by temporary liquidity problems, need emergency liquidity support systems to come to their rescue. Similarly, UCBs classified in Grade III and IV with meagre or entirely eroded net worth needs solvency support for their revival. Representatives from the UCB sector, during the meeting with the Working Group emphasized the need for addressing these pressing issues.

The Working Group, while appreciating the need for evolving a mechanism to address the aforesaid twin issues, is of the view that it should not be the mandate of the Umbrella Organization to provide such emergency liquidity and solvency support to UCBs as it may be difficult for it to meet the quantum of financial assistance that may be required in this regard. Further, solvency support is subject to high risk and low or nil return and envisages a fairly long period of pay back. Neither the sector, nor the Umbrella Organization, being a non-deposit taking NBFC, would be in a position to fund the recapitalization needs of problem UCBs. However, arrangements need to be put in place to address and resolve these problems.

K. Emergency Liquidity Support: The Working Group believes that due to lack of homogeneity, uneven geographical spread of UCBs, cultural differences, affinity to state federations and state laws on co-operation, the bonding of UCBs at the State level is strong. Empirical evidence also demonstrates that the contagion effects are localized and solidarity amongst the co-operatives at the State level is far greater than at the national level. The emergency liquidity supports need to be provided to UCBs in financial distress and, in most cases, such facility would be without collateral and for a short term. The uncollateralized emergency liquidity support would carry more than the normal counter party credit risk. Therefore, a thorough understanding of the local polity, the management and operations of the distressed UCB, its problems and prospects would be necessary. The Working Group is of the view that a State level institution would not only have better appreciation of the financial needs of the distressed UCB, but also pull resources for supporting the UCB concerned. Therefore, the Working Group recommends State-specific Emergency Fund Facility Schemes.

L. Revival Fund: The presence of a large number of weak and sick UCBs (about 399; 23 percent of the total), which need solvency support, call for an urgent need for creation of a Revival Fund. If UCBs with negative net worth were to be brought to positive net worth, an enormous sum of about ₹ 2,500 crore may be required. While RBI may pursue a menu of options, including mergers, with or without DICGC support, and financial restructuring for turn around of these banks, possibly, an amount of ₹ 2,000 crore may still be necessary. However, such a fund could only be raised out of contribution from the net profits of UCBs. The total net profit of the sector being about ₹ 1,000 crore, mobilization of this magnitude of resources from the sector may not be feasible. The Working Group has observed that though the Central/State Governments have been supporting the revival of the rural co-operatives, such support was not extended to UCBs. Therefore, in the absence of capital contribution from the Central/State Governments, the Revival Fund for solvency support to UCBs would not be feasible. The Working Group also believed that the providing solvency support to UCBs from contributions from the profits may be resisted by the sector and the contribution would be too little to rescue sick UCBs. Therefore, it would be more appropriate to provide both short and medium term finance from the Emergency Fund. UCBs not complying with the prescribed CRAR may be supported from the Emergency Fund by way of subscription to Tier II instruments issued by these banks.

To sum up, it is significant to note that introduction of reforms and the consequent increase in competition has resulted in some convergence in operations of commercial banks and co-operative banks, especially scheduled UCBs. Furthermore, while most of the loss-making commercial banks are relatively small, in the case of UCBs some of the large banks are incurring losses and this has increased the vulnerability of the whole segment. Detection of irregularities in a few UCBs in the recent past has raised concerns about the conduct of the management in co-operative banks. For this purpose, the RBI has suggested the establishment of a unified supervisory authority for UCBs and the related amendment to the Banking Regulation Act, 1949.

5

Co-operative Banks in Europe

5.1 Nature and Importance

Co-operative banks have always been a vital motivating force behind the financing and development of the economies of European countries.

They form part of the *co-operative societies* whose role in Europe is recognized and encouraged by EU institutions, as evidenced in the recent statute of the "European Co-operative Society" and the European Commission communication on the "promotion of co-operative societies in Europe".

Even if the co-operative traditions and legislations differ from one European country to another (as do some of the characteristics of co-operative banks themselves) there are nonetheless several substantial common factors at the heart of the European co-operative banking sector. The principal one is that they function democratically. European co-operative banks belong to their members, who participate in their democratic management, according to the principle: *one person, one vote*. It is similarly important to emphasize that co-operative banks are decentralized networks established at a local level.

As a result, the primary mission of co-operative banks is to promote the economic interests of their members, who are also their customers. In other words, their principal aim is to create value for their "*members/customers*", by furnishing them with quality products, at best prices, and by supporting the economic and social integration of individuals.

By their origin and nature, co-operative banks have historically been leaders in supplying financial services adapted to certain categories of customers, such as farmers and small and medium-sized enterprises (SMEs) to whom access to credit at other banks is limited. About 32 percent of small and medium-sized European businesses, representing a total of 4.2 million, are co-operative bank customers. Co-operative banks provide a fully comprehensive banking service to the personal segment whose customer base in Europe totals more than 130 million.

Co-operative banks are integrated into their local environment and their role goes beyond that of the provider of financial services. By coordinating grants and other resources at local level and applying them for their designated purpose, they play a key role in the development of regional and local economies and of social cohesion.

Co-operative banks operate today in a competitive market, *on a level playing field* with commercial banks. They have more than demonstrated their ability to actively contribute to recent changes in the sector. As major players in the financial sector, co-operative banks contribute to its stability and competitiveness, thanks to their sound capitalization, their low-risk profile, and the consistency of their performance. The excellent ratings obtained in recent years, based on *the quality of their assets and their healthy financial profiles,* confirm and validate their contribution to the stability of financial markets and banking systems.

The nature and importance of co-operative banks, the potential that their presence represents for society, are not always understood and their position is sometimes misrepresented. There is sometimes even confusion between co-operative banks and savings banks or public banks. Furthermore, there is a tendency to paint the entire group of co-operatives with the same brush. The confusion persists despite the fact that several studies have identified the key explanatory factors of the role and the competitive advantages of co-operative banking organizations.

Firstly, co-operative banks are private ventures *subject to the same legal framework as all other banks*, in conformity with banking directives. Likewise, they are subject to the same rules of risk management and the same supervisory authorities.

Secondly, co-operative banks are fully subject to market regulations, either directly because they float stocks invested with shareholders, or indirectly because they have a vehicle quoted on the stock exchange.

Lastly, shares subscribed by members/customers *are remunerated*. This remuneration can take the form of preferential interest rates, of rebates, of favourable tariffs for services rendered, or more generally, of dividends. In no way, therefore, does the unique status of co-operative banks contravene with free market regulations.

As a general rule, co-operative banks in Europe do not benefit from any preferential treatment regarding taxation. Furthermore, co-operative banks do not enjoy any kind of monopoly on savings and credit products, subsidised capital or government guarantees, except for a few exceptions that are offset by constraints.

Co-operative banks do not enjoy unfair price advantages over commercial banks. The possibility of offering products at preferential prices is closely linked to their capital structure, held by the member customers—which allows for reductions in costs and an efficient business model—and to the primary mission of co-operatives, which is to maximize customer value. For this reason, co-operative banks stimulate efficiency and competition in the banking sector. It is thereby rendered more competitive, which is a positive contribution.

Co-operative status does not permit hostile takeovers that, more often than not, are doomed to failure, as genuine consent of the members is needed. This highlights a fundamental of co-operative banking and the application of one of the principles of corporate diversity and, of economic democracy (it is the members/clients who decide the bank's fate). Co-operative is a form of organization generally recognized among the member States, and has at its disposal all appropriate legal rights and powers to permit the development of its activities internally and across all frontiers.

Does it, nonetheless, represent an obstacle to the process of consolidation of the European banking sector. It must be realized that a process of consolidation does not exclusively, or even principally, emerge on the strength of takeover bids, partnership agreements, sub-contracting and outsourcing, resource pooling, the formation of joint subsidiaries, etc., which are among the numerous options on offer. Co-operative banks have often been a driving force behind consolidation, nationally.

The acquisition of co-operative banks by non-co-operative institutions is not impossible, and some concrete examples of it have taken place, as in Italy and in Belgium. Moreover, a number of major commercial banks are today part of financial groups controlled by co-operative banks, thus contributing to the consolidation of the European banking industry. Furthermore, a listed stock company has at its disposal, a wide range of means to protect itself from hostile takeovers (i.e. syndicate agreements, different types of holding interests in stock companies and political interference in acquisition of domestic banking institutions).

Some of Europe's leading commercial banks resort to this practice as a matter of course. As a general rule, it is useful to bear in mind that the ultimate reason for financial consolidation and integration is *to promote a more efficient allocation of available resources* within the European economy, for the benefit of customers. It is thus a question of effecting economies of scale and range in the banking industry in order to achieve improved efficiency and competitiveness. Hence, considering the perspectives and structures of the markets in Europe (which are fundamentally different from those prevailing in the United States) are cross-border mergers—really the only practical means of arriving at an efficient allocation of resources?

The available economic literature on the subject of economies of scale, as well as on the effects of banking mergers, particularly in the retail banking segment, does not lead to any clear conclusions in its presentation of different and contradictory empirical results for a good number of countries and for different time periods.

In this respect, co-operative banks have improved their efficiency in different ways: (a) by greater integration of local and regional banks; (b) by centralizing information systems and a number of support functions; (c) at an international level, by promoting cross-border alliances and cooperation (UNICO, CIBP, or the subsidiaries created by Natexis and DZ Bank aimed at developing and exploiting joint assets); and (d) by their decentralized network *organisation*, which allows for the allocation of tasks—for example, outsourcing, to reduce operating costs.

5.2 Co-operative Banks and European Economies

Co-operative banks bring significant contributions to the European economy. They contribute to the efficiency of the banking system and therefore of the economies.

Presently, co-operative banks operate in highly competitive markets. They do so, successfully by applying the co-operative principles underlying their business model. Owned by members/customers, their primary mission is to offer them the best services, as opposed to maximizing of profit for the shareholders. Profits are nevertheless necessary to ensure the durability and development of the enterprise. Taking account of this unique approach to the market and of their structural characteristics, co-operative banks are in a position to offer services that correspond to customers' needs, while maintaining their concern for fair prices. On account of their proximity to their members and their firm establishment locally, co-operative banks are well placed to gather more comprehensive information on their customers, and at a lower cost. This permits them to *evaluate the needs and the solvency of their customers more thoroughly than other banks.* The information asymmetry is reduced and thus moral hazard and adverse selection may be lowered.

Consequently, co-operative banks are able, on the one

hand, to achieve a generally *superior credit allocation* to that of the overall banking system and on the other hand to supply products and services tailored to customers' real needs, at best prices. Competition with other players is thereby intensified, which, in turn, improves efficiency and competitiveness for the entire banking sector, and ultimately for the economy.

Co-operative banks also contribute to the performance of the European economy, by the financial support that they bring to all economic units, notably the SMEs, farmers, families, professionals, and residents of rural or outlying zones who, thanks to the presence of co-operative banks, can have full access to credit.

Because of their close links with the SMEs, for whom they represent the major source of financing, co-operative banks also work towards the creation of enterprise and innovation, thus contributing to a competitive and growing economy.

In a nutshell, co-operative banks, by their specific legal status and organizational system, represent a unique form of enterprise which co-exists with other forms such as commercial banks or savings banks, and which ensures an appropriate response to the *diversity of market needs.*

This pluralistic approach to the economy and its players, one of the components in a competitive spirit, is the cornerstone of an efficient and competitive market, as opposed to one based on standardization, concentrations and monopolies.

5.2.1 Accessible and High-Quality Service: Co-operative banks have been the yardstick for *efficient business management* based on democratic principles. They encourage the active participation of their members/customers in the strategic evolution of a company, thus taking their place in a long-term perspective for the banking activity. Unlike other companies quoted on the stock exchange, the management of co-operative banks is not subject to the volatility of financial markets. This approach reflects equally positively on the relationship between customer and bank. The long-term interests of customers are crucial to the activity of co-operative banks, regardless of their current circumstances.

Co-operative banks are in a position to collect and bring together pertinent information concerning *the expectations and needs of the customer.* Thus, they are particularly well placed to adapt their products and services, resulting in a *high level of customer satisfaction.*

For the same reason, co-operative banks have had exceptional success in anticipating market needs, thus playing a leading innovative role in the area of both products and technology. The concept of bank insurance (*bancassurance*) created by the French co-operative banks following the Crédit Mutuel in the 1970s and 1980s, or the recent successes in the field of electronic banking recorded by the Finnish Okobank, the Dutch Rabobank, and the Austrian RZB (which played a pioneering role amongst new member countries in this sector), are examples among numerous others of the innovative force of the co-operatives.

In short, the *business model* of co-operative banks also ensures a *high degree of consumer protection,* since not only are customers well informed, they also, as members, play an active part in decision-making.

5.2.2 Active Intervention at Local Level: Co-operative banks, as decentralized networks, are deeply involved in their local environment. Historically, they were created by groups, by local communities, to compensate for the absence of easily accessible banking services, and as a consequence they have evolved in the context of these communities. For this reason, notions of social cohesion and solidarity are at the very heart of co-operative banking.

Nowadays, co-operative banks offer a strong impetus to local economic dynamism, particularly through their financing of agriculture, local community and SMEs, and by the promotion of social integration or educational programmes. What is more, they are substantial employers and often the prominent taxpayers in their region. The long-term view of co-operative banks allows them to foster values which go well beyond a simple financial return. Underlining this approach, co-operative banks are pioneers in the field of sustainable development and corporate social responsibility—a priority to which their competitors have only recently directed their attention.

5.2.3 Reinforcing Stability of Financial Systems: Co-operative banks are characterized by strong capitalization (high solvency ratio), by moderate risk levels, and stable profit levels, as emphasized in the reports by Standard & Poor's (S&P), Fitch and by FMI. The FMI report in particular points out that co-operative banks act as a buffer against any crisis in the banking system.

The S&P report equally highlights their regulatory function: "co-operative banks have demonstrated their capacity to consistently produce operational results, such a capacity being linked to their minimum involvement in more volatile transactions".

With regard to the New Agreement on Capital Stock or Basel II, the European co-operative banks lower the pro-cyclical effects of internal ratings, thanks to their high solvency ratios. What is more, their model is of decentralized decision-making, permitting efficient and healthy risk management.

Finally, because of their financial robustness, co-operative banks reinforce the stability and competitiveness of (and therefore confidence in) the European financial system.

5.2.4 Allocation of Resources: Co-operative banks contribute significantly to the general efficiency of the economic system, thereby refuting the assertion that they are inefficient and lacking in innovation. The fact that the working coefficients of the co-operative banks are today comparable to those of commercial banks, operating in the same market, bears out the point. Another factor to be considered is whether cost and efficiency are the only criteria with which to evaluate the performance of banking enterprises.

With regard to innovation, the European co-operative banks have shown themselves to be leaders in numerous fields. The examples of one-stop-shopping (bancassurance) in France and the electronic bank (efficient distribution) in Finland and Holland have already been mentioned. The "customer value" orientation and the ownership structure are key innovative factors at the heart of the co-operative banking system.

5.2.5 Profitability of the Banking System: The presence of co-operative banks in a market generally ensures relatively favourable loan rates for customers. However, co-operative banks must be careful to respect the criteria for profit, since their capitalization depends mainly on earnings put in reserves. In any case, the presence of co-operative banks results in *growing competition* and a banking system that is consequently more efficient and more competitive, and not the reverse. What is more, it is consistent with the very nature of co-operative banking: promoting the economic progress of the members/clients, by supplying them with the entire range of financial services and at the same time ensuring the long-term viability and development of the bank.

The assertion that the margins and therefore the results or the return on equity are too weak in the countries where co-operative banks dominate the market, seem equally without foundation. The benefits for members cannot be measured uniquely in terms of dividends paid or *profits*. The "*returns*" for members also takes the form of growth of SMEs, of housing conditions, of local development, of what is known as "surplus" ("leftover stock") for customers, and the general level of confidence in the market. The fact that these "*returns*" are difficult to quantify in monetary terms should not lead us to ignore them. With regard to the assertion that co-operative banks cause other banks to leave the market, it should be noted that not only is there no proof of such a tendency, but what is more the leading banks in the European market are introducing development strategies into new markets throughout Europe. Finally, their level of capitalization and their low-risk profile constitute stabilizing forces in the banking industry.

To sum up, the banking sector in Europe is characterized by equality in the conditions of competition, in a market where different business models co-exist. The co-operative model gives proof of its efficiency, recognized moreover by the stakeholders and makes a substantial contribution in terms of competitiveness and stability to the European economies and financial markets. The co-operative model is dominant in all that concerns corporate democratic governance and social responsibility in business, and in terms of the capacity to respond to customer needs.

An in-depth analysis of European co-operative banks shows that their success is due to their philosophy, democratic organizational structure and their capacity to respond to the needs of the market. For this reason, it is important to publicize the reality and values of co-operative banks as well as their contribution, through the quality of their services, to the objectives of economic and social development, of competitiveness, and of employment.

6

Co-operative Banks in Select Countries

6.1 Rabo Bank Group of Netherlands

Taking its cooperative basis as a starting point, Rabobank Group puts the common interests of people and communities first. Based on its commitment to those interests, Rabobank Group aims to be a driving, innovating force that contributes to the sustainable development of prosperity and well-being. The goal is to help people and communities achieve their current and future ambitions. Supplying the best possible financial solutions and strengthening mutual collaboration are the means to achieve that end. As part of this mission, Rabobank Group wants to be the most customer-oriented and innovative financial institution in the Netherlands.

At the international level, Rabobank Group aspires to be the best food and agribusiness bank, with a strong presence in the world's major food and agriculture countries. To this end, Rabobank Group harnesses the knowledge and experience it has accumulated in the Netherlands and many other countries over the years. Rabobank Group also wants to achieve global excellence in sustainable banking—as befits a bank with its identity and position in society.

6.1.1 Co-operative Goals: The cooperative structure means specifically that Rabobank Group's first and foremost duty is to serve the interests of its customers by: (a) providing those financial services considered best and most appropriate by its customers; (b) ensuring continuity in services with a view to protecting the long-term interests of its customers; and (c) showing commitment to its customers and their environment, so that it can can help them achieve their ambitions.

Rabobank's cooperative structure and local ties have set it

apart for over 110 years. The 139 local Rabobanks and their more than 7.6 million customers, including their 1.9 million members, form the heart of the cooperative. The local Rabobanks, for their part, are members and shareholders of Rabobank Nederland, the umbrella co-operative that advises the branches and supports their local services. The structure of Rabobank Group is typified by strong mutual relationships originating in its co-operative roots, even though the subsidiaries and associates are not structured as co-operatives themselves.

Pursuant to the Dutch Financial Supervision Act, Rabobank Nederland monitors aspects such as operations, solvency, liquidity and outsourcing at the local Rabobanks. In addition, Rabobank Nederland acts as the holding company of a number of specialist Dutch and foreign subsidiaries. Rabobank Nederland has an employee base of about 6,800 FTEs. Including foreign subsidiaries, Rabobank International has an employee base of some 15,800 FTEs. Rabo Development supports the advancement of a banking infrastructure in seven countries, which includes developing countries, by taking non-controlling interests in rural banks and offering them expertise and human capital. Rabobank Foundation helps vulnerable and underprivileged groups in and outside the Netherlands to participate in society by contributing funds, human resources and knowledge.

Rabobank's roots lie in agriculture. In 1898, two separate co-operative banks—the Coöperatieve Centrale Raiffeisen Bank in Utrecht and the Coöperatieve Centrale Boerenleenbank in Eindhoven—were founded by enterprising rural folk, who, with little access to the capital market, decided to help one another.

6.1.2 Rabobank International: Although Rabobank International was only formally established in 1996, international activities have long been part of that history. Rabobank International slowly came into existence over the course of the 1970s—when Rabobank's business customers began to express a growing demand for services abroad. In response to a clear need for international banking services, Rabobank opened branch offices in Europe, North America, Asia and South America and entered into strategic alliances with European partners. It also purchased existing foreign banks (such as ADCA in Germany and PIBA in Australia, ACC in Ireland and the Valley Independent Bank in the US), enabling Rabobank to take its expertise in the field of consumer banking and the agricultural sector to promising markets abroad.

6.1.3 The Idea of Raiffeisen: The idea of Raiffeisen served as the inspiration for the establishment of agricultural co-operative banks in the Netherlands. Friedrich Wilhelm Raiffeisen founded the first agricultural co-operative bank in Germany in 1864. As a rural mayor, he witnessed first-hand, the poverty some suffered within the farming community. He set up a charitable foundation in order to provide relief. However, he gradually came to the conclusion that self-help was more beneficial than charity in order to bring about lasting improvements. This led him to transform his charitable organisation into a farmers' co-operative bank in 1864. This 'Heddesdorfer Darlehnskassen-Verein' collected the savings from the rural population so as to be able to fulfil the local need for credit. The fundamental principles of the co-operatives were: self-help, self-responsibility and self-management.

From the late 1890s, there were many followers of the Raiffeisen co-operative movement in the Netherlands. One of the first was the priest Gerlacus van den Elsen. He initiated a number of local agricultural co-operative banks in the southern part of the Netherlands. His mission was both exalted and down-to-earth. In his own words: 'To fend off usury, to stand by the farmer in his time of need, and also to encourage thriftiness, charity, industriousness and moderation'.

6.2 Germany

The co-operative financial system in Germany dates back

to the 19th century. In order to allow small craftsmen, merchants, and farmers to have access to credit and the banking system, co-operative financial institutions were developed. In Germany, urban craftsmen and merchants were served co-operatively by *volksbanken*. Agrarian interests were served by *raiffeisenkassen*. Almost from the beginning, local *volksbanken* and *raiffeisenkassen* formed co-operative central banks to assist them in managing their liquidity. The separate central banking systems for the *volksbanken* and the *raiffeisenkassen* were ultimately supported by the development of a third tier designed to assist the co-operative central banks manage their liquidity. This third tier was founded in 1895 as the predecessor to DG Bank.

In addition, in 1972, the *volksbanken* and *raiffeisenkassen* formed a national federation (separate and distinct from their financial collaboration through DG Bank) called the Bundesverband der Deutschen Volksbanken und Raiffeseinbanken (the "BVR"), to which all of their regional federations belong. This distinction between the financial association and the trade association is similar to the distinction made in France between the CNCA and the FNCA and in Quebec between the confederation and the caisse centrale. In some areas of Germany (namely, the southwest of Germany, including Stuttgart, Frankfurt am Main, and Dusseldorf), the *volksbanken* and the *raiffeisenkassen* have retained their second tier co-operative central banks, which, in turn, are served by DG Bank. In most of the rest of Germany, local *volksbanken* and *raiffeisenkassen* do not have a co-operative central bank.

They obtain their wholesale financial products and services directly from DG Bank, making this part of the German cooperative financial system, a two tier system.

There are approximately 2,400 local co-operative banks in Germany with consolidated assets of DM438 billion. Together with DG Bank's own 21 branches, the co-operative credit sector serves Germany with more than 16,000 domestic branches.

The German co-operative financial system comprises approximately 2,400 local *volksbanken* and *raiffeisenkassen*. A person need not be a member of a local co-operative bank in order to obtain financial products or services. The German co-operative financial system has approximately 14 million members, but has over 30 million customers.

The local co-operative banks offer the widest possible array of financial services, including insurance products, leasing, and securities trading. Many of the products and services available to customers are developed by DG Bank or by its subsidiaries. Each of the local co-operative banks is restricted by its articles of association to a geographic trading area. This ensures that there is no competition between local co-operative banks and a rational distribution of service outlets. Deposits in local co-operative banks are guaranteed as to 100 percent by the mutual assurance of all of the local and regional banks and DG Bank. There is no pre-funded deposit insurance reserve fund. As a result, there is not annual premium cost to the banks.

6.2.1 Central Co-operative Banks and Regional Federations: The three regional banks provide their member local banks with liquidity management, including deposits and liquidity loans. They participate with their members in syndicated loans and generally support the local banks with backroom processing and international services, as required. These services are available on a "user-pay" principle. Liquidity is attracted to the central co-operative banks on a voluntary basis. Local banks are entitled to invest their liquidity in any qualifying instrument. The central co-operative banks compete in the open market for local bank deposits. In Germany, employee training is given a high priority. The regional federations and the BVR and its regional offices deliver training and development to employees of the local and central banks.

In addition, the regional federations execute the external audit and inspection functions on behalf of the regulator and the member/shareholders. The stabilization fund which assists in recapitalizing underperforming local banks is also managed at the regional federation level. DG Bank and the BVR, regardless of whether a *volksbanken* or a *raiffeisenkassen* comes from a three tier region or a two tier region, the DG Bank is positioned to provide services to it. In fact, DG Bank is the national focal point for the German co-operative financial services system. DG Bank divides its business into three divisions.

6.2.2 Customer Divisions, Product Divisions and Service Divisions: The DG Bank serves local banks which do not have a central co-operative bank with all of their backroom processing. It provides liquidity to those local banks and offers liquidity loans. It provides clearing and settlement to the local banks directly and through their central co-operative banks. It is important to note that DG Bank is the international point of contact for the German co-operative banking sector. It has established many international offices to serve its international customers based in Germany. Further, it is positioned to participate in international money markets to assist it in its role as the focal point for clearing and settlement on behalf of the group. DG Bank's international services provide significant profits which assist in the delivery of products and services to its member/customers at reasonable prices and helps provide a financial margin to generate dividends for member/ shareholders.

It is interesting to note that notwithstanding the lack of an express cross guarantee structure in the DG Bank group, the DG Bank issues a form of internationally traded debt, which is unique in the area of financial services. So-called "covered bonds", are debt instruments which are secured by a revolving pool of assets on which the holders of the bonds have a preferred claim.

6.2.3 Organization, Governance, and Decision Making: Except for the fact that the local co-operative banks are co-operatives and that DG Bank is a joint stock company, their organization and governance structures are identical.

The inter-relationship among the DG Bank, the central co-operative banks, and the local banks was severely tested in the early 1990s. As a result of significant losses due to interest rate mismatches, the DG Bank, due to demands from regulatories, required additional capitalization from the central and local co-operative banks to the tune of US$ 875 million. The recapitalization was successful.

6.2.4 Volksbanken and Raiffeisenkassen: At the local level, the *volksbanken* and the *raiffeisenkassen* are organized and operated on co-operative principles. No share capital is invested. Each of the local co-operative banks capitalize themselves through retained earnings. Members elect the supervisory board (usually around 8 or 10 people) which appoints a board of directors of three people. It is the board of directors of the local banks which are the directing minds of the local bank and are held accountable for its financial performance. The supervisory board monitors their performance, but also ensures that the local banks maintain strong links with the local communities, especially small and medium enterprises and agricultural businesses, and works to ensure that the local bank's products and service delivery are designed to serve its community's unique needs. The local banks (and the entire system) pride themselves on fast decision making, close contact with their customers and trusting business relationships and believe that it is these qualities in addition to sound financial management which makes DG Bank group a success.

6.2.5 DG Bank: DG Bank is not a co-operative. It is a joint stock company. The capital stock of DG Bank is mainly held by the central co-operative banks or the local co-operative banks (approximately 80 percent, 45 percent held by local banks and more than 30 percent held by central co-operative banks). Other shareholders include co-operatives and co-operative associations. Participation in a central co-operative bank or in DG Bank is voluntary. Those who participate agree to provide guarantees of solvency and liquidity to DG Bank, which makes the same guarantees to other financial institutions on behalf of the *volksbanken* and the *raiffeisenkassen*.

The supervisory board of the DG Bank consists of 32 persons. Over half of the board is made up of representatives from the local and regional banks and the BVR. The federal government controls three seats on the board, the state governments (the "*landers*") control 3 and the Bundesbank places one representative on the board. Other directors come from the minority owners, the non-financial co-operatives and agricultural interests. The president of the supervisory board is always the president of the BVR, the trade association for the German co-operative banks.

Decision-making with the elimination of all but three of the central co-operative banks, the DG Bank developed a series of regional head offices. This approach was designed to create a means for linking the local banks directly with the DG Bank. Each local bank was allocated to a regional head office and, as part of the regional head office, an elected advisory committee was formed. Input from the local banks is, therefore, accumulated at DG Bank's regional head offices and communicated down the line to DG Bank's headquarters in Frankfurt.

Votes on issues of strategic policy take place at the DG Bank annual general meeting. This meeting is attended by all of the shareholders, including local banks which directly own equity in DG Bank and the central co-operative banks which own equity in DG Bank on behalf of their members. Even though a number of local banks are represented by their local co-operative banks, all local banks are entitled to attend the DG Bank annual general meeting. Generally, votes on money issues are decided on a one-vote per share basis. Non-money issues are normally decided on a one-member, one-vote basis.

6.2.6 Regulatory Environment: Although Germany is a federal state, all levels of the co-operative financial system are federally regulated as co-operative banks under German federal banking law. The German Bundesbank (the German central bank) requires that all local and regional co-operative banks and that DG Bank itself maintain a deposit at the Bundesbank @ 2.5 percent of their assets as liquidity reserves. Deposits in the Bundesbank do not earn interest. In the two-tier part of the system, the DG Bank applies regulatory, monitoring and supervision over the local banks. In the three-tier part of the system, this aspect of self-regulation is managed by the central co-operative banks.

In either case, where a local bank suffers financial difficulty or is poorly managed, the DG Bank or the regional centrals intervene to ensure that the local bank's difficulties are managed and resolved. In the same way, the DG Bank supervises the operations of the central co-operative banks and exercises the same level of supervisory management over the central cooperative banks.

6.3 France

6.3.1 Background: Credit Agricole, which is a three-tier system of co-operatively operated and organized financial institutions, is acknowledged to be, in the aggregate, France's largest bank in terms of market share, earnings (US$ 2.1 billion, for fiscal 1998), and total capital. Its total assets as on December 31, 1998 were US$ 455.5 billion. Credit Agricole was founded at the local level in 1894 to serve France's farming community. The French Republic recognized the spontaneous private farmer initiatives in many areas of the country which had as their goal the provision of credit for farmers. By the turn of the century, the local caisses developed a need for a regionally based second tier and, as a result, during this time, the Caisses Regionales was incorporated.

In 1920, the national government of France established the Caisse Nationale de Credit Agricole (CNCA), the third tier, as a public agency/crown corporation aimed at: (i) reinforcing the unity of the local and regional caisses which formed the Credit Agricole group; (ii) controlling the operations of the local and regional caisses; and (iii) enhancing the availability of credit to the people of France. State "sponsorship" through the CNCA and through favourable legislative and financial rules, solidified the strong financial footings upon which the Credit Agricole group is founded.

In 1988, CNCA was transformed into a privately-owned joint-stock corporation. The French government sold its holdings to the regional caisses (approximately 90 percent) and to the employees of the Credit Agricole group (approximately 10 percent). La Federation Nationale du Credit Agricole (FNCA) is a trade association separately incorporated from the CNCA.

It is important to note that state sponsorship for over 60 years led to a strong centralized model. During those 60 years, the chief executive officer of the CNCA was a government appointee, who was charged with ensuring that credit was available to agricultural interests. A large proportion of the deposits raised in local communities was, during this time, deposited with the CNCA for reallocation to communities as part of government policy. Despite the fact that CNCA was privatized in 1988, the culture of the Credit Agricole group is, therefore, quite different from any other co-operative financial institution.

6.3.2 Business:

A. Local Caisses: At the local level, there are 2,775 local caisses with 5.5 million member shareholders consisting primarily of individuals, farmers, and agricultural co-operatives. The local caisses have evolved to become co-operative holding companies for the regional caisses. Their only asset is their investment in their regional caisse. The local caisses no longer play a direct role in providing financial services. The members of the board of directors of these caisses represent community interests and ensure that the regional caisse respond to the need for special products and services for their local customers/members. The directors take a role in promoting Credit Agricole in their communities.

Even though the local caisses are not operating banks, a position on the board of directors is still considered prestigious in the culture of the local communities they serve.

Regional caisses will confer with the board of directors of a local caisse on credit decisions relating to local small and medium enterprises or agribusinesses.

B. Regional Caisses: The role of delivering financial services to members and customers has been assumed by the 57 larger regional caisses, which manage multi-branch operations throughout their assigned region of France. The largest regional caisse is the Credit Agricole de Paris with approximately FF100 billion. While the business of the regional caisses was originally focused on the agricultural sector, beginning in 1959, the Credit Agricole group diversified its lending activity and progressively became a universal bank. Credit Agricole group's current portfolio of loans reflects the gradual change in its business—personal loans: 40 percent; international corporate clients: 22 percent; small and medium enterprises: 12 percent; agriculture: 12 percent; professionals: 8 percent and local communities: 7 percent. The 57 independent regional caisses operate a network of 8,200 branches. Each regional caisse provides a comprehensive range of banking products and financial services which are standardized through the direction of the CNCA, thus ensuring uniformity of image and policy from one region of France to another and from on regional caisse to another. Each regional caisse operates within a defined geographic territory. A person need not be a member in order to obtain products or services from a regional caisse. Credit Agricole group has 5.5 million people who are members of the local caisses, with over 15.5 million customers.

Competition between the regional caisses is eliminated by agreements among the regional caisses and the CNCA to restrict business to the territory defined by CNCA. These agreements are reflected in the articles of association of the regional caisses. Each regional caisse generally sells the products and services developed by CNCA, although there is no formal mandatory rule to do so. In practice, decisions coming from the CNCA are generally adhered to because the CNCA consults with its members before acting and because by centralizing the administration of many of its services to regional caisses, the CNCA is able to capitalize on economies of scale and offer the best pricing to the caisses regionales, who would otherwise be able to buy products and services in the open market at much greater cost. All deposits up to FF 450,000 are insured by mutual commitments from banks in France to cover those deposits in the event of a bank failure. There is no government operated deposit insurer and no pre-funded deposit insurance reserve fund.

C. CNCA: As the central body of the Credit Agricole group as prescribed by French law, CNCA balances four main roles: (i) central bank, treasury, and liquidity manager for the regional caisses; (ii) holding company for the Credit Agricole's group of financial service providers (investment banking, corporate banking, fund management, payment systems, leasing, and insurance); (iii) develops and coordinates the implementation of strategy and direction for the Credit Agricole, including the regional caisses; and (iv) regulates the regional caisses to ensure that each regional caisse maintains satisfactory levels of liquidity and solvency.

6.3.3 Organization, Governance, and Decision-making Structures: Credit Agricole prides itself on combining a decentralized decision making structure and a unified financial and commercial approach.

A. **Local Caisses:** There are approximately 2,770 local caisses. A typical local caisse represents a defined geographic area with a population of approximately 25,000. It will have some 2,000 member/stockholders who will be entitled to vote to elect the thirteen person board of directors.

In total, there are over 35,000 French citizens who serve on the boards of the local caisses.

B. Regional Caisses: The regional caisses are generally

capitalized through investments by the local caisses and their retained earnings. The local caisses expect to be paid a return on their investments in their regional caisses so that they, in turn, can pay a dividend to their members. Over the past decade, eighteen regional caisses have obtained funding in the capital markets by issuing non-voting preferred shares (certificats cooperatifs d'investissement) that are traded in the stock markets. Holders of these shares expect a market rate of return on their invested capital.

While generally non-voting, these shares give the holders certain rights upon default and in fundamental changes in the regional caisse (e.g., merger). Each regional caisse is owned by a group of local caisses from the region who meet to elect the regional caisse's board of directors. Each regional caisse is a company in itself, owned by the group of local caisses in their region, administered by the elected board of directors who appoint a professional management team to run the business. Regional caisses have board of directors of between 12 and 15 people. These directors are elected at annual general meetings.

All of the directors from the local caisses attend the annual general meeting of a regional caisse and each of them casts a vote in director elections and in other matters coming before the general meeting. Special meetings are called from time to time to deal with issues of importance or urgency.

C. CNCA: Majority ownership of CNCA is held by the regional caisses. The regional caisses appoint delegates and along with the other shareholders, the employees, elect a board of directors of 15 persons, composed of: (i) eight chairs of the regional caisses; (ii) three chief executive officers of the regional caisses; (iii) three directors representing the employees; and (iv) one representative from the agricultural community. CNCA is not a co-operative. It is a joint stock company under French corporate law. Nevertheless, the CNCA recognizes that its owners are its customers and, as a result, recognizes the necessity of consulting with its members on matters of importance or urgency. The CNCA maintains a number of standing committees on major issues, such as retail banking products and services, small and medium enterprise, and computer connectivity, which meet on a monthly basis to provide input to CNCA management in their areas of expertise.

France has a unitary government structure. The local caisses, the regional caisses, and the CNCA are all incorporated and regulated pursuant to French banking laws, which is specifically designed for co-operative banking structures.

French banking laws establish liquidity, solvency, and administrative and management rules for all three levels of the Credit Agricole group. Through authority delegated to it by the Bank of France, the CNCA exercises regulatory authority over its regional caisses, particularly in the area of liquidity, solvency, and governance.

Because of the strong linkages between the operations of the regional caisses and their interdependence through a cross guarantee structure which culminates with the CNCA, the CNCA exercises considerable influence over the operations of the regional caisses over and above legislated rules and procedures.

A major part of the management of the liquidity and solvency of the interdependent regional caisses involves enforcing capital adequacy and liquidity standards.

6.4 Kenya

The first legislation to specifically govern the registration of co-operatives—Co-operative Societies Ordinance—was enacted. Kenya Co-operative Creameries (KCC) became the first co-operative to be registered on 8th February 1931. This was followed shortly by Kenya Farmers Association (KFA) in 1931, the Kenya Planters Co-operative Union (KPCU) in 1937 and the Horticultural Co-operative Union (HCU) in 1951. However, the 1931 Ordinance did not allow Africans to participate in co-operatives.

Due to the need to bring about a more efficient and effective co-ordination of both internal and external assistance in addition to providing relevant financial services to the co-operative movement, the Government considered the idea of setting up of a co-operative bank during 1964. It is deemed necessary to conduct a survey to ensure the bank is set on sound footing.

As a result of initiative and advice of KNFC, a group of people from the Department of Co-operative Development visited Israel to study ways and means of establishing a viable co-operative bank. The same year, a joint paper by the Ministry of Finance and Marketing and Co-operatives Development recommending the establishment of the bank was issued.

Two Israeli experts also sent their recommendations to the Government to that effect. The Government accepted the recommendations and made arrangements to have established banks to support it. Consequently, an official from Standard Chartered D.G. Landells was appointed General Manager to assist with the establishment of the Co-operative Bank of Kenya Limited.

The co-operative movement witnessed a structural change with the formation of the Kenya National Federation of Co-operatives (KNFC) as an apex body to promote the interest of the co-operative movement as a whole.

Co-operative Bank of Kenya was registered as a co-operative society on 19th June 1965. It did not however commence operations as it was not registered under the Banking Act. In this status, it could fulfil the main objective for its establishment, which was to mobilise financial resources and provide banking services to the co-operative movement. The Bank applied for a banking license to operate under the Banking Act, which was granted later in 1968.

The Co-operative Bank opened for business on 10th January 1968 with a modest capital base of Kes 255,000. The

Government supplemented the capital with a Kes 214,000 interest-free loan repayable in 10 years. The Banking Act, however, required banks to have a minimum capital of a 'staggering' Kes 2 million. The Government granted an exemption and offers a grace period within which the required capital was to be raised.

The Commissioner for Co-operative Development, with the support of KNFC, was obliged to direct that all co-operative society funds invested with other banks be transferred to the Co-operative Bank. The Commissioner further advised that all co-operatives should buy shares in the Bank. This tremendously increased the bank's deposit and capital base, laying a firm foundation for the bank.

During 1994, the Bank converted itself to become a full-fledged commercial bank offering the complete range of financial services beyond the captive co-operative sector to include personal, corporate and institutional customers.

The Bank also listed on the Nairobi Stock Exchange on December 22, 2008. The listing followed a public offer of 701.3 million shares at Kshs 9.50 which achieved an 81 percent subscription to raise Kshs 5.4 billion in additional capital on top of the existing Kshs 7.4 billion. This was made possible as the bank's special general meeting on 27th June approved conversion of the Bank to a limited liability company from a co-operative society that it has been since its inception in 1965. All previous shares held by the Co-operatives were ring-fenced under the Co-op Holdings Co-operative Society Limited which became a strategic investor in the bank with a controlling 65 percent stake.

6.5 USA

The National Consumer Cooperative Bank (NCCB), the parent body of The National Cooperative Bank was created and chartered by the National Consumer Cooperative Bank Act (92 Stat. 499, 12 U.S.C.A. 3001), enacted on August 20, 1978. The bank is directed by the act to encourage the development of new and existing co-operatives. The bank provides specialized credit and technical assistance to eligible co-operatives that provide goods, services, housing, and other facilities to their members as ultimate consumers. The bank is itself structured as a cooperative financial institution. Under its congressional charter, the bank is directed to make loans and offer its services throughout the United States, its territories and possessions, and the Commonwealth of Puerto Rico.

The Act provided that the federal government would contribute the initial capitalization of the bank through the purchase of the bank's Class A stock. All 15 members of the bank's board of directors are appointed by the president of the United States. The Act contemplated that the number of president-appointed directors was to decrease gradually as borrowers and co-operatives eligible to borrow purchased Class B and Class C stock in the bank.

In 1981, the Act was amended by Title III, subtitle C, of the Omnibus Budget Reconciliation Act of 1981 (95 Stat. 433). The 1981 Act converted the federal government's initial capitalization of the bank, formerly represented by Class A stock, into Class A capital notes, held by the secretary of the treasury. The Act further mandated that after the Final Government Equity Redemption Date (FGERD), as defined by the National Consumer Cooperative Bank Act, the bank's Class B and C stockholders would elect 12 of the bank's 15 directors. The remaining three were to be appointed by the president with the advice and the consent of the Senate. The president is directed by the Act, as amended, to select one member from among proprietors of small business concerns, one member from among the officers of the agencies and departments of the United States, and one member from among persons having extensive experience in the co-operative field representing low-income eligible co-operatives.

The bank is operated by a board of directors under bylaws and policies it prescribes, consistent with the National Consumer Cooperative Bank Act.

The bank's credit and technical assistance to co-operatives

is intended to improve the quality and availability of goods and services to consumers. The bank makes loans to eligible co-operatives at prevailing market interest rates.

The bank encourages broad-based ownership, control, and active participation by members in eligible co-operatives. The bank also seeks to maintain broad-based control of the bank by its voting stockholders.

The National Consumer Cooperative Bank Act established the Office of Self-Help Development and Technical Assistance within the bank. Co-operatives that are eligible to receive assistance from the bank may be eligible to qualify for financial and technical assistance from the office. The office may provide financial assistance to newly developed or established co-operatives that cannot qualify for a bank loan, or when the membership of the co-operative consists substantially of low-income persons or it provides services to low-income persons.

The Omnibus Budget Reconciliation Act of 1981 directed that as soon as practical after the FGERD, the board of directors of the bank would establish a non-profit corporation under the laws of the District of Columbia to succeed the office and to carry out the functions of the office. That non-profit corporation, the Consumer Cooperative Development Corporation, was incorporated on December 30, 1982.

In 1985, the NCCB became a private financial institution and changed its name to National Cooperative Bank (NCB). At the same time, the Consumer Cooperative Development Corporation became the NCB Development Corporation (NCBDC). In 1986, the NCB registered with the Securities and Exchange Commission and performed its first private placement. The NCB, in 1995, launched the Community Association Loan Program that provided financing for condominium, townhouse, and other owner associations. By 2000, the NCB had provided more than US$ 6 billion in financing to homes, school facilities, assisted living units, and other community developments.

National Cooperative Bank (NCB) provides comprehensive banking services to co-operatives and other member-owned organizations throughout the country. What makes NCB unique is that the bank was created to address the financial needs of an underserved market niche—people who join together co-operatively to meet personal, social or business needs, especially in low-income communities.

NCB's customers are co-operatives, such as grocery wholesaler co-ops, purchasing co-ops or housing co-ops. Other customers share in the spirit of co-operation, driven by democratic organizing principles. They may be Alaska and Native American enterprises, which by their very nature, are member-run and member-owned. Others may be community health centres or charter schools, driven entirely by community needs. What they all have in common is a single fundamental principle—they have joined together co-operatively to meet personal, social, and/or business needs.

6.6 Bangladesh

The origin of Grameen Bank can be traced back to 1976 when Professor Muhammad Yunus, Head of the Rural Economics Program at the University of Chittagong, launched an action research project to examine the possibility of designing a credit delivery system to provide banking services targeted at the rural poor. Grameen Bank (GB) has reversed conventional banking practice by removing the need for collateral and created a banking system based on mutual trust, accountability, participation and creativity. GB provides credit to the poorest of the poor in rural Bangladesh, without any collateral. At GB, credit is a cost effective weapon to fight poverty and it serves as a catalyst in the overall development of socio-economic conditions of the poor who have been kept outside the banking orbit on the ground that they are poor and hence not bankable. Professor Muhammad Yunus, reasoned that if financial resources can be made available to the poor people on terms and conditions that are appropriate and reasonable, "these millions of small people with their millions of small pursuits can add up to create the biggest development wonder".

As of October, 2011, it had 8.349 million borrowers, 97 percent of whom were women. With 2,565 branches, GB provides services in 81,379 villages, covering more than 97 percent of the total villages in Bangladesh.

The Grameen Bank Project (Grameen means "rural" or "village" in Bangla language) came into operation with the following objectives:

1. Extend banking facilities to poor men and women.
2. Eliminate the exploitation of the poor by money lenders.
3. Create opportunities for self-employment for the vast multitude of unemployed people in rural Bangladesh.
4. Bring the disadvantaged, mostly the women from the poorest households, within the fold of an organizational format which they can understand and manage by themselves.
5. Reverse the age-old vicious circle of "low income, low saving and low investment", into virtuous circle of "low income, injection of credit, investment, more income, more savings, more investment, more income".

The mode of operation of Grameen Bank is as follows. A bank branch is set up with a branch manager and a number of centre managers and covers an area of about 15 to 22 villages. The manager and the workers start by visiting villages to familiarise themselves with the local milieu in which they will be operating and identify the prospective clientele, as well as explain the purpose, the functions, and the mode of operation of the bank to the local population. Groups of five prospective borrowers are formed; in the first stage, only two of them are eligible for, and receive, a loan.

The group is observed for a month to see if the members are conforming to the rules of the bank. Only if the first two borrowers begin to repay the principal plus interest over a period of six weeks, do the other members of the group become eligible themselves for a loan. Because of these restrictions, there is substantial group pressure to keep individual records clear. In this sense, the collective responsibility of the group serves as the collateral on the loan.

Loans are small, but sufficient to finance the micro enterprises undertaken by borrowers: rice-husking, machine repairing, purchase of rickshaws, buying of milk cows, goats, cloth, pottery etc. The interest rate on all loans is 16 percent. The repayment rate on loans is currently 95 percent due to group pressure and self-interest, as well as the motivation of borrowers.

Although mobilization of savings is also being pursued alongside the lending activities of the Grameen Bank, most of the latter's loanable funds are increasingly obtained on commercial terms from the central bank, other financial institutions, the money market, and from bilateral and multilateral aid organizations.

Grameen Bank credit delivery means taking credit to the very poor in their villages by means of the essential elements of the Grameen credit delivery system.

Grameen Bank credit delivery system has the following features:

1. There is an exclusive focus on the poorest of the poor. *Exclusivity is ensured by*:

(a) Establishing clearly the eligibility criteria for selection of targeted clientele and adopting practical measures to screen out those who do not meet them.

(b) In delivering credit, priority has been increasingly assigned to women.

(c) The delivery system is geared to meet the diverse socio-economic development needs of the poor.

Borrowers are organized into small homogeneous groups: Such characteristics facilitate group solidarity as well as participatory interaction. Organizing the primary groups of five members and federating them into centres has been the foundation of Grameen Bank's system. The emphasis from the very outset is to organisationally strengthen the Grameen clientele, so that they can acquire the capacity for planning and implementing micro level development decisions. The Centres are functionally linked to the Grameen Bank, whose field workers have to attend Centre meetings every week.

Special loan conditionality which are particularly suitable for the poor, include:

1. Very small loans given without any collateral.
2. Loans repayable in weekly instalments spread over a year.
3. Eligibility for a subsequent loan depends upon repayment of first loan.
4. Individual, self chosen, quick income generating activities which employ the skills that borrowers already possess.
5. Close supervision of credit by the group as well as the bank staff.
6. Stress on credit discipline and collective borrower responsibility or peer pressure.
7. Special safegaurds through compulsory and voluntary savings to minimise the risks that the poor confront.
8. Transparency in all bank transactions most of which take place at centre meetings.
9. Simultaneous undertaking of a social development agenda addressing basic needs of the clientele.

This is reflected in the "sixteen decisions" adopted by Grameen borrowers. This helps to:

1. Raise the social and political consciousness of the newly organized groups.
2. Focus increasingly on women from the poorest households, whose urge for survival has a far greater bearing on the development of the family.
3. Encourage their monitoring of social and physical infrastructure projects—housing, sanitation, drinking water, education, family planning, etc.

The system has evolved gradually through a structured learning process that involves trials, errors and continuous adjustments. A major requirement to operationalize the system is the special training needed for development of a highly motivated staff, so that the decision-making and operational authority is gradually decentralized and administrative functions are delegated at the zonal levels downwards.

As the general credit programme gathers momentum and the borrowers become familiar with credit discipline, other loan programmes are introduced to meet growing social and economic development needs of the clientele. Besides housing, such programmes include:

1. Credit for building sanitary latrines.
2. Credit for installation of tube wells that supply drinking water and irrigation for kitchen gardens.
3. Credit for seasonal cultivation to buy agricultural inputs.
4. Loan for leasing equipment/machinery, i.e., cell phones purchased by Grameen Bank members.
5. Finance projects undertaken by the entire family of a seasoned borrower.

The Grameen Bank's Method of action can be illustrated by the following principles:

1. Start with the problem rather than the solution: a credit system must be based on a survey of the social background rather than on a pre-established banking technique.
2. Adopt a progressive attitude: development is a long-term process which depends on the aspirations and commitment of the economic operators.
3. Make sure that the credit system serves the poor, and not vice-versa: credit officers visit the villages, enabling them to get to know the borrowers.
4. Establish priorities for action vis-à-vis to the target population: serve the most poverty-stricken people needing investment resources, who have no access to credit.
5. At the beginning, restrict credit to income-generating production operations, freely selected by the borrower. Make it possible for the borrower to be able to repay the loan.

6. Lean on solidarity groups: small informal groups consisting of co-opted members coming from the same background and trusting each other.
7. Associate savings with credit without it being necessarily a pre-requisite.
8. Combine close monitoring of borrowers with procedures which are simple and standardised as possible.
9. Do everything possible to ensure the system's financial balance.
10. Invest in human resources: training leaders will provide them with real development ethics based on rigors, creativity, understanding and respect for the rural environment.

Every year, GB staff evaluates their work and check whether the socio-economic situation of GB members is improving. GB evaluates poverty level of the borrowers using ten indicators.

A member is considered to have moved out of poverty if her family fulfils the following criteria:

1. The family lives in a house worth at least Tk. 25,000 (twenty five thousand) or a house with a tin roof, and each member of the family is able to sleep on bed instead of on the floor.
2. Family members drink pure water of tube-wells, boiled water or water purified by using alum, arsenic-free, purifying tablets or pitcher filters.
3. All children in the family over six years of age are all going to school or finished primary school.
4. Minimum weekly loan instalment of the borrower is Tk. 200 or more.
5. Family uses sanitary latrine.
6. Family members have adequate clothing for every day use, warm clothing for winter, such as shawls, sweaters, blankets, etc., and mosquito-nets to protect themselves from mosquitoes.
7. Family has sources of additional income, such as vegetable

garden, fruit-bearing trees, etc., so that they are able to fall back on these sources of income when they need additional money.

8. The borrower maintains an average annual balance of Tk. 5,000 in her savings accounts.
9. Family experiences no difficulty in having three square meals a day throughout the year, i.e. no member of the family goes hungry any time of the year.
10. Family can take care of the health. If any member of the family falls ill, family can afford to take all necessary steps to seek adequate healthcare.

6.6.1 How is Grameen Bank Different from Conventional Banks? Grameen Bank methodology is almost the reverse of the conventional banking methodology. Conventional banking is based on the principle that the more you have, the more you can get. In other words, if you have little or nothing, you get nothing. As a result, more than half the population of the world is deprived of the financial services of the conventional banks. Conventional banking is based on collateral—Grameen system is collateral-free.

Grameen Bank starts with the belief that credit should be accepted as a human right, and builds a system where one who does not possess anything, gets the highest priority in getting a loan. Grameen methodology is not based on assessing the material possession of a person—it is based on the potential of a person. Grameen believes that all human beings, including the poorest, are endowed with endless potential.

Conventional banks look at what has already been acquired by a person. Grameen looks at the potential that is waiting to be unleashed in a person.

Conventional banks are owned by the rich, generally men. Grameen Bank is owned by poor women.

Overarching objective of the conventional banks is to maximize profit. Grameen Bank's objective is to bring financial services to the poor, particularly women and the poorest—to help them fight poverty, stay profitable and financially sound. It is a composite objective, coming out of social and economic visions.

Conventional banks focus on men; Grameen gives high priority to women. 97 percent of Grameen Bank's borrowers are women. Grameen Bank works to raise the status of poor women in their families by giving them ownership of assets. It makes sure that the ownership of the houses built with Grameen Bank loans remain with the borrowers, i.e. the women.

Grameen Bank branches are located in the rural areas, unlike the branches of conventional banks which try to locate themselves as close as possible to the business districts and urban centres. First principle of Grameen banking is that the clients should not go to the bank, it is the bank which should go to the people instead. Grameen Bank's 22,124 staff meets 8.35 million borrowers at their door-step in 81,379 villages spread out all over Bangladesh, every week, and deliver bank's service. Repayment of Grameen loans is also made very easy by splitting the loan amount in tiny weekly instalments. Doing business this way means a lot of work for the bank, but it is a lot convenient for the borrowers.

There is no legal instrument between the lender and the borrower in the Grameen methodology. There is no stipulation that a client will be taken to the court of law to recover the loan, unlike in the conventional system. There is no provision in the methodology to enforce a contract by any external intervention.

Conventional banks go into 'punishment' mode when a borrower is taking more time in repaying the loan than it was agreed upon. They call these borrowers "defaulters". Grameen methodology allows such borrowers to reschedule their loans without making them feel that they have done anything wrong (indeed, they have not done anything wrong.)

When a client gets into difficulty, conventional banks get worried about their money, and make all efforts to recover the money, including taking over the collateral. Grameen system, in such cases, works extra hard to assist the borrowers in difficulty, and makes all efforts to help him/her regain his/her strength and overcome difficulties.

In conventional banks, charging interest does not stop unless specific exception is made to a particular defaulted loan. Interest charged on a loan can be multiple of the principal, depending on the length of the loan period. In Grameen Bank, under no circumstances total interest on a loan can exceed the amount of the loan, no matter how long the loan remains unrepaid. No interest is charged after the interest amount equals the principal.

Conventional banks do not pay attention to what happens to the borrowers' families as results of taking loans from the banks. Grameen system pays a lot of attention to monitoring the education of the children (Grameen Bank routinely gives them scholarships and student loans), housing, sanitation, access to clean drinking water, and their coping capacity for meeting disasters and emergency situations. Grameen system helps the borrowers to build their own pension funds, and other types of savings.

Interest on conventional bank loans are generally compounded quarterly, while all interests are simple interests in Grameen Bank.

In case of death of a borrower, Grameen system does not require the family of the deceased to pay back the loan. There is a built-in insurance programme which pays off the entire outstanding amount with interest. No liability is transferred to the family.

In Grameen Bank, even a beggar gets a special attention. A beggar comes under a campaign from Grameen Bank which is designed to persuade him/her to join Grameen programme. The bank explains as to how she can carry some merchandise with her when she goes out to beg from door to door and earn money, or she can display some merchandise by her side when she is begging in a fixed place. Grameen's idea is to graduate her to a dignified livelihood rather than continue with begging.

Such a programme would not be a part of a conventional bank's work.

Grameen system encourages the borrowers to adopt some goals in social, educational and health areas. These are known as "Sixteen Decisions" (no dowry, education for children, sanitary latrine, planting trees, eating vegetables to combat night-blindness among children, arranging clean drinking water, etc.). Conventional banks do not see this as their business.

6.6.2 Grameen Bank II: Grameen Bank has come a long way since it began its journey in the village of Jobra in 1976. During this quarter of a century it has faced many operational and organisational problems and has gained a lot of experience through its successes and failures. It incorporated many new features in its methodology to address various crisis and problems, or utilise new opportunities; discarded and modified the features which became unnecessary or less effective. There were a number of major natural disasters in Bangladesh during the life span of Grameen Bank. The 1998 flood was the worst of all. Half of the country was under flood-water for ten long weeks. Water flowed over the roof-tops for a prolonged period.

Grameen borrowers, like many other people of Bangladesh, lost most of their possessions including their houses because of the flood. Grameen Bank, which is owned by the borrowers, decided to take up a huge rehabilitation program by issuing fresh loans for restarting income-generating activities and to repair or rebuild their houses. Soon borrowers started to feel the burden of accumulated loans. They found the new instalment size exceeding their capacity to repay.

When the repayment situation did not improve as desired, the GB thought this would be a good opportunity to be bold, and to dare to design a new Grameen methodology, incorporating all the lessons learnt, and the wishes and the desires that the GB accumulated during the quarter century of

Grameen's operation. The designing process formally began on April 14, 2000 (Bengali New Year's day). Field-testing began immediately. By the beginning of 2001, the new system, "The Grameen Generalised System" or GGS was ready for launching to manage the transition from the Grameen Classic System (GCS) to GGS in 41,000 villages without subjecting hundreds of thousands of illiterate borrowers to a big shock, and messing up the accounts in 1,175 branches.

Transition was very carefully and meticulously choreographed, and put into action by March 2001. By April, 2002, two years after GB began the process, Grameen Bank II emerged. The transition is now complete. The last branch of Grameen Bank switched over to Grameen II on August 7, 2002, completed the process of transition. The new Grameen Bank II is now a real and functioning institution. This second generation micro credit institution appears to be much better equipped than it was in its earlier version.

In the Grameen Bank II, gone are the general loans, seasonal loans, family loans, and more than a dozen other types of loans; gone is the group fund; gone is the branch-wise, zone-wise loan ceiling; gone is the fixed size weekly instalment; gone is the rule to borrow every time for one whole year, even when the borrower needed the loan only for three months; gone is the high-level tension among the staff and the borrowers trying to steer away from a dreadful event of a borrower turning into a "defaulter", even when she is still repaying; and gone are many other familiar features of Grameen Classic System.

7

International Associations/Institutions of Co-operative Banks

7.1 International Co-operative Banking Association (ICBA)

The International Co-operative Banking Association (ICBA) is a sectoral organisation of the International Co-operative Alliance (ICA). The ICBA was set up in 1922 by national co-operative banks and financial organisations. The ICBA's mission is to contribute to the sound development, growth and competitiveness of co-operative banks in the marketplace by defending their interests and by promoting worldwide their important contribution to the economic and social well-being of the population and their communities.

As a global organisation for co-operative banks, it has four key aims:

1. To facilitate the promotion at the international and regional levels of the distinctive co-operative values of co-operative banks and of the advantages of using them over other banks.
2. To facilitate and encourage the exchange of information amongst members on key co-operative banking issues and foster inter-cooperation in the finding of solutions.
3. To support regional committees and their members, individually or collectively with specific challenges.
4. To encourage inter-cooperation with other types of co-operatives and various bodies of the ICA.

The ICBA Central Executive maintains close contact with the World Council of Credit Unions (USA), the European Association of Co-operative Banks (Brussels) and the International Raffeisen Union (Bonn). The ICBA is a true global and democratically elected Specialised Organisation of the ICA, representing the views of co-operative financial institutions all over the world.

7.1.1 Structure of ICBA: The ICBA's Board is the Executive Committee, whose members enjoy a four year term of office. The President is elected from those members. Also, there are Regional Committees (each with a Regional Chairperson). The Regional Chairpersons are all vice-presidents and members of the Central Executive Committee and are indicated on the Central Executive members list. The remaining members of the Central Executive represent their organisation directly and can decide whether also to become a member of their Regional Committee.

7.1.2 Statutory Meetings: The Central Executive Committee meets in Spring and Autumn, although it can convene meetings at other times as necessary. Its Plenary Session is also held in the Autumn in conjunction with the meeting of the Central Executive Committee. Ideally, each of the Regional Committees should meet at least three times a year.

7.1.3 Membership of ICBA: Membership for the ICBA is invited from national and international co-operative banks with a good reputation, a democratic constitution, affiliated to the ICA, and those institutions which are interested in co-operative banking affairs, provided that their objects are in conformity with the objectives of the ICA.

7.1.4 ICBA Activities: ICBA organises statutory meetings as well as thematic seminars to address specific issues for co-operative financial institutions. In addition, it publishes a journal and e-bulletin.

The ICBA activities include:

1. The organisation of statutory meetings (including two executive committee meetings).
2. The holding of a yearly seminar in conjunction with one of it statutory meetings.
3. The publication of a journal to include the annual seminar presentations.
4. The provision of relevant member information and

newsworthy material.

5. Upon request of members, the meeting with and/or lobbying national or international groups and authorities.

7.1.5 Past Activities:

1. **2004 Seminar:** The ICBA Seminar addressed the theme, "Mission and Role of Co-operative Banks in the Sphere of Economy and Finance" in Warsaw (Poland) in September 2004.
2. **2003 Seminar:** ICBA held a seminar on the subject of "Challenges of Co-operative Banks facing Globalisation and Concentration in Financial Markets" in September in Oslo (Norway). Participants included leaders of co-operative banks and co-operators attending the ICA General Assembly. Speakers included the President of ICBA's Regional Committees and the Chairpersons of Norwegian Land kredit.
3. **ICBA Executive Meeting, 2003:** An important meeting of ICBA Executive Committee was held between August 31 and September 1 2003 in Oslo (Norway), where members accepted the foundations of ICBA's marketing and lobbying plan for 2004 and beyond.
4. **Meeting of Members of the ICBA Executive Committee and ICBA European Regional Committee, 2003:** A meeting of members of Executive Committee and European Regional Committees of ICBA as well as the Presidium of European Association of EU Co-operative Banks was held on April 22 2003 in Warsaw, Poland. Participants of the meeting are also invited to the international conference on the "Role and Assignments of Co-operative Banks in the Economic Transformation of Poland and its Accession to European Union" jointly organised by the National Association of Co-operative Banks and the Main School of Trade of Warsaw which took place April on 24-25, 2003 in Warsaw.
5. **Central Executive Committee, 2002:** Following meeting of Executive Committee ICBA held on October 9, 2002 in

Lisbon, Portugal, one of the major decisions of the meeting was the election of new Chairman of ICBA, Mr. Eugeniusz Laszkiewicz, Chairman of Board of National Association of Co-operative Banks of Poland. Also agreed was the move of the ICBA Secretariat to the National Association of Co-operative Banks in Warsaw, Poland.

7.1.6 Planned Activities: ICBA proposes to initiate a major data gathering operation aiming at promoting co-operative banking groups, on a worldwide scale, as major economic players whose distinctive socio-economic mission and humanistic values contribute greatly to the health and vitality of local communities and populations.

This project called upon the co-operation of other associations of financial co-operatives such as the EACB (European Association of Co-operative Banks) and others and called upon ICBA's regional chapters for collecting data. It namely drew some material from the current EACB project of praising co-operative banks' values and advantageous commercial practices but complement it to give it an international scope.

The project should enable to portray co-operative banking groups as an attractive option for consumers of banking services who wish for a more humane globalisation. It should expose the types of special benefits provided by co-operative banks, their humanistic values, the social aspect of their mission, their contribution to sustainable local development as well as to job creation and preservation.

The gathering of the information mentioned above should be complemented by key testimonials of world leaders and businesses who believe in the co-operative formula and can bring concrete proof of its relevance and importance in today's world. The exact form that would take the final product needs to be discussed. Nevertheless, the promotional information could be made available to the ICBA members, members of the co-operative banks' international community and members of the ICA to serve various purposes, nationally and internationally.

7.2 European Association of Co-operative Banks (EACB)

It has been the voice of Europe's co-operative banks since 1970. It represents, promotes and defends the common interests of its 28 member institutions and of co-operative banks in general. Co-operative banks form decentralised networks which are subject to banking as well as co-operative legislations. With 4,200 locally operating banks and 63,000 outlets, co-operative banks are widely represented throughout the enlarged European Union, playing a major role in the financial and economic system. In their long tradition, they have served 160 million customers, mainly consumers, SMEs and communities. Europe's co-operative banks represent 50 million members and 7,50,000 employees and have an average market share of about 20 percent. In some countries, such as Austria, Germany, Finland, France, Italy and the Netherlands, the market share is well above this figure, ranging from 30 percent to 50 percent.

7.2.1 Mission Statement: The European Association of Co-operative Bank is committed to defending and promoting co-operative values and the interests of its members within a competitive environment that allows co-operative banks to best serve their members and clients. To this end, the Brussels-based organisation provides information and advice, and contributes to the dialogue between European institutions and stakeholders.

7.2.2 Promoting Co-operative Values: The organisation supports and promotes the values of the co-operative movement in European and international institutions—central to these values are the principle of democracy—with the principle of "one person-one vote" at its core; a strong commitment to social values; and links with 59,000 bank branches—as an alternative to "shareholder value" and financial markets-oriented institutions.

7.2.3 Delivering Value-added Services: The EACB's workshops, seminars, publications and information allow its members and other co-operative organisations to increase their awareness and knowledge of European issues, keep them up to date with legislative and regulatory developments and offer a platform to develop co-operation between the members.

7.3 World Council of Credit Unions (WOCCU)

World Council of Credit Unions (WOCCU) is the leading international trade association and development agency for credit unions. Since 1971, WOCCU has increased access to high quality financial services worldwide by strengthening credit unions using a well defined and thoroughly tested development model. Member-owned and established at the grassroots, credit unions are sustainable financial intermediaries that serve a broad base of members from all income and wealth levels.

In addition to offering innovative technology solutions, WOCCU's technical assistance programs equip credit unions and other types of financial co-operatives with the tools and techniques necessary to strengthen their financial management and deliver fairly priced financial services to large numbers of poor and low-income people. Unlike many microfinance technical assistance providers that focus exclusively on credit, WOCCU's approach emphasizes the mobilization of member savings as the primary source of financing. This savings-based approach allows credit unions to reach great scale in financial service provision and instils a level of financial discipline that ensures long-term sustainability.

At the second-tier level, WOCCU builds national credit union networks that enable safe and sound institutions to reach greater efficiencies of scale, employ new technologies and provide a broader array of services and service points to members. WOCCU also works closely with credit union leaders, national government officials and policy makers to create appropriate and effective regulatory environments for credit unions.

WOCCU has a long and successful history working with multinational, bilateral and private partners to develop and strengthen member-owned credit unions and their national/regional systems around the world. WOCCU has implemented more than 275 long- and short-term technical assistance programs with funding from various donors, such as:

1. Asian Development Bank (ADB).
2. Bill and Melinda Gates Foundation.
3. Consultative Group to Assist the Poor (CGAP).
4. Financial Sector Deepening (FSD) Trust.
5. Inter-American Development Bank (IDB).
6. U.K. Department for International Development (DFID).
7. U.S. Agency for International Development (USAID).
8. U.S. Department of Agriculture (USDA).
9. World Bank.
10. National governments.
11. Worldwide Foundation for Credit Unions.

WOCCU's technical assistance methodology achieves results in a variety of operating environments, placing high priority on employing innovative technology solutions and transferring knowledge to local credit union staff.

WOCCU's three-phase model for strengthening credit unions and increasing access to financial services on a mass scale, results in the provision of affordable, available and accessible financial services.

WOCCU's core capabilities are grounded in its drive to provide millions of poor and low-income people access to the array of financial services they need through credit unions, regardless of challenges posed by the surrounding environment. Most recently, WOCCU has proven its capabilities meet this mission in eight key areas:

1. Partnerships and alliances.
2. Networking.
3. Transaction services—payments, remittances, cards.
4. IT systems.

Phase III both broadens and deepens outreach by enabling

credit unions to pool resources to procure new technology and create a wide network of service access points.

WOCCU combines the fundamentals of financial services with new technology to help credit unions reach poor people in rural and remote areas ignored by other financial institutions. In all cases, WOCCU assesses the local climate and develops an outreach strategy based on local demand and available resources.

In Bolivia, WOCCU helped credit unions establish profitable new branches in remote areas and worked at the sector level to bring ATM access to rural areas and advocate for a sound regulatory framework for micro finance.

In Mexico, WOCCU developed a successful methodology to take both group-based and individual savings and loan products to poor members in some of the most marginalized areas of the country, so that members no longer have to travel long distances to access savings and loans.

WOCCU worked with rural credit unions in Peru to introduce financial products tailored to the needs of small producers and vendors along value chains to help bring products to market and encourage fair commercialization.

In Afghanistan, where WOCCU built a credit union system from the ground up, credit unions offer members financial products and services compliant with Islamic law.

Recognizing the critical role credit unions play in reaching the underserved, the Bill and Melinda Gates Foundation awarded WOCCU funding to establish and test an application service provider (ASP) for small credit unions in Kenya. The ASP, or data centre, provides back-office software solutions to credit unions that cannot afford it on their own.

WOCCU offers the following services:

7.3.1 Developing Integrated Business Networks: In addition to strengthening individual institutions, WOCCU helps credit unions band together to build national business networks that enable them to reach greater efficiencies of scale, employ new technologies and provide a broader array of services to members. In countries such as Bolivia, Guatemala, Ecuador, Nicaragua and Rwanda, the standard-driven networks create a unified national presence for credit unions.

The technology-driven networks developed by WOCCU in Bolivia and Ecuador provide the architecture for centralized data storage that enables services such as liquidity pooling, reinvestment and deposit insurance among credit unions, as well as bill payment, national and international shared branching, remittance distribution, ATM networks, card services and mobile services for members.

7.3.2 Offering Domestic and International Remittances: WOCCU's international remittance network offers credit unions in the United States, Kenya and Latin America access to money transfer networks for originating and distributing remittances. Transactions flow through the infrastructure of established money transfer operators with which WOCCU has partnered. Credit unions offer the services on both the sending and receiving sides in regions with high levels of migration.

Credit unions do much more than offer more affordable options for sending money. Recognizing the potential of remittances for attracting unbanked clients as future savers and borrowers, credit unions invite both members and non-members to send and receive remittances. WOCCU has worked with partner credit unions in Latin America to develop remittance-linked savings and credit products.

7.3.3 Rebuilding during and after Conflicts: In communities torn apart by conflict, the community-based credit union may be the only institution that people still trust because of its ability y to meet their basic needs for access to finance. WOCCU's approach to technical assistance has proven to be adaptable and successful in conflict and post-conflict areas.

In Afghanistan and Colombia, WOCCU has increased credit union outreach in areas, still experiencing fighting. In Sri Lanka, WOCCU is strengthening credit unions in areas affected by the conflict with the intent of restoring financial stability and a broader sense of security. In Macedonia and Rwanda, WOCCU improved credit union financial performance while bringing people of different ethnicities together to rebuild their communities through credit unions.

7.3.4 Supporting Communities at Risk: As trusted organizations in their communities, credit unions are effective vehicles for supporting communities at risk. In Kenya, WOCCU worked through credit unions on peer-to-peer training to raise awareness, share information and mitigate the spread of HIV/AIDS through prevention. Taking an integrative approach to stemming further spread of the disease, WOCCU provided vulnerable and affected households with labour-saving devices and offered education savings accounts for adolescents affected by the disease.

7.3.5 Reconstructing after Disaster: When disaster strikes, access to financial services is critical for people to rebuild their lives; credit unions provide that access. In Sri Lanka, WOCCU worked with local credit unions to rebuild after the 2004 tsunami. WOCCU also supported disaster relief and rebuilding through credit unions after Haiti's earthquake in 2010.

7.3.6 Establishing New Credit Union Systems: Experienced with both grassroots organizing and engaging in dialogue with national governments to ensure that credit unions are permitted to operate, WOCCU has built credit union systems from the ground up in countries like Afghanistan and Uzbekistan. Taking local customs, religious beliefs and traditional practices into account, WOCCU helps credit unions develop products and services tailored to the local environment to meet the needs of members and potential members. In countries where credit unions do not exist, WOCCU begins by building strong individual institutions and then links them together via a national business network to achieve economies of scale.

7.3.7 Encouraging Legislative Reform and Regulatory System Development: WOCCU works directly with credit unions and national governments to develop laws and regulations that support safe and sound credit union systems. To that end, WOCCU has developed a model credit union law, an international comparative analysis of credit union legislation and model regulations that are available online and by request.

WOCCU has worked directly with governments in countries as diverse as Ecuador, Kenya, Mexico, the Solomon Islands and Uzbekistan to provide technical assistance in legislative reform and regulatory system development. WOCCU also supports healthy regulatory environments by helping credit unions develop the capacity to advocate for appropriate legislation on the national level and comply with standards once established.

8

Problems and Future Challenges for Co-operative Banks

8.1 No Final Owners

Co-operative banks face challenges rooted in their institutional set up. Most co-operatives were designed to perpetually accumulate capital, by limiting both members' ownership rights and profit distribution. As a result, the economic value of a co-operative, net of debts and the nominal value of member shares, constitutes an inter-generational endowment without final owners.

In some ways, this endowment is akin to a foundation, meant to benefit a class of people. It is available for use by current members, with the understanding that they will grow it and pass it on to the next generation of members, with co-operative bank managers as custodians.

Because the members have only a fixed-value claim on the co-operative, their incentive to exert effective oversight over management is lower than that of shareholders in a joint-stock company. As co-operatives get bigger, ordinary members become one class of stakeholder, while managers and employees emerge as new stakeholders with interests that are not necessarily aligned with those of the other members (often employees are also owners). That means the need for member oversight of management can increase even as the incentive to do so declines.

Moreover, in a standard investor-owned institution, control is proportional to ownership and larger shareholders can be expected to take an oversight role to protect their investment. In a one-member, one-vote arrangement, the incentive to vote is low for the average member. But for those owners with a direct stake in the institution's behaviour, such as borrowers and employees, there is a much increased incentive to vote, in favour of policies that are beneficial to them.

8.2 Reduced Market Discipline

In general, the consumer surplus of borrowers exceeds the consumer surplus of savers. Reduced market discipline and often lower disclosure requirements can also hinder governance, resulting in a higher risk of imperilling the endowment.

While most co-operative banks are small, they are often part of networks that centralize certain business functions to reap economies of scale and scope and provide financial backstops for any member co-operative that faces problems. The degree of operational integration within these networks differs significantly—from very limited to so extensive that the network in effect constitutes an integrated banking group. The trend has been towards greater integration.

Networks may include checks and balances that reduce governance problems at individual cooperatives, but the governance of a network as a whole constitutes a new challenge. With increased integration and centralization, managers and board members at individual co-operatives face conflicting incentives. They are supposed to oversee the centre while being dependent on it for their own success and in many cases being subject to oversight by the centre.

8.3 Co-operative Banks and Financial Stability

What do co-operative bank ownership and the competitive dynamics between co-operative and commercial banks imply for financial stability? By pursuing objectives other than profit maximization, co-operative banks could increase the fragility of financial systems. In particular, they could deliver financial services at below-market prices, at the expense of both their own capitalization and the profitability and soundness of competing banks.

Difficulties in adjusting to adverse circumstances and

raising capital could render co-operatives more vulnerable to extreme shocks. Also, their focus on traditional bank lending to members, whose characteristics usually are similar, tends to imply relatively large and correlated exposures to credit risk. On the other hand, co-operative banks generally have lower incentives to take on risks.

The z-score soundness measure—which estimates the likelihood that a company will run out of capital on the basis of its capitalization, profitability, and the volatility of its returns—indicates that co-operative banks tend to be more stable than commercial banks. This is because of the much lower volatility of co-operatives' returns, which more than offsets their lower profitability and capitalization.

8.4 Mutual Support Mechanisms

This lower return volatility may result from the fact that in normal times co-operative banks pass on most of their returns to customers as consumer surplus (offering them better deals, so to speak, than they can get elsewhere). But in weaker periods, they are able to retain these returns. To some extent, the mutual support mechanisms within networks of co-operative banks may also reduce volatility.

But the econometric estimates also suggest that a higher presence of co-operative banks tends to significantly reduce the soundness of weak commercial banks in the same financial system. This can be explained by the fact that a higher presence of retail-focused co-operative banks tends to push commercial banks towards less stable revenue sources such as corporate banking or investment banking.

Overall, though, a higher presence of co-operative banks appears to have a slightly positive impact on the stability of the banking sector as a whole.

8.5 Cost of Service in Co-operative Banks

Cost of service in banks is different from the concept of "Economics of Branch Banking". Cost of banking service is related to the cost of individual transactions and such cost to the customers. These are related to the bank charges for various types of bank services charged by the banker. A banker must charge reasonable amount for banking operations like cheque operations, mail transfers, issuing drafts, honouring cheques etc. When banking operations are heavy, there is scope for reduction in the cost of service. If the banking operations are less, then there is a possibility to have higher cost of service. Some of the means through which cost of banking services could be reduced by a co-operative banker are cited below:

1. **Staff Selection:** While selecting the employees for a single co-operative bank, employees with prior experience must be recruited or for banks with branches; newly recruited employees should not be sent to new branches. Employees with adequate experience must be recruited. They must be given adequate training prior to their appointment, especially when they are sent for rural branches.
2. **Better Salary and Working Conditions:** Co-operative banks world over, with exceptions, have an image of poor salary payers. This image must be erased and they must pay competitive market salary for their employees. By paying a reasonable market-oriented salary, the efficiency of the employees will increase. Employees' efficiency will definitely save time of banking operations and reduce the cost of banking services.
3. **Steps to Add More Services:** To reduce the cost of banking services, co-operative banks must introduce new and innovative banking services. Apart from normal banking services, innovative banking services to suit the local needs and conditions must be explored by cooperative banks. Sometimes regular banking services may not be sufficient to use the fuller potential of employees. Co-operative banks may think of adding additional services like agency services on behalf of

Government, municipal organizations, NGOs etc. They can sell bonds, debentures and related securities and can add time and service utility. E-banking, tele-banking services, ATM service etc. could also be introduced. They could also add additional income through such transactions. They can also make arrangements to receive tax payments from the customers. Even payment of insurance premium could be facilitated to the customers through cooperative banks.

4. **Reducing Formalities:** One of the ways through which cost of service could be reduced is to reduce banking formalities of filling up number of forms or vouchers by customers. Simplifying such formalities will not only rescue cost of operations, but also save the time of customers. The banker could reduce the cost on stationeries and printing. Such simplification of formalities and banking procedures is possible by means of arranging discussions with the employees and with other bankers.

8.6 Introduction of Automation/Mechanisation

Technology is changing fast in all fields of activities. Through technological changes and innovations, we can save lot of time, energy and resources. Such technological changes are fast spreading in the banking field also. Co-operative banks have to catch up with such situation and they should not lag behind commercial banks. Modern banking facilities are to be mixed with internet and web-based services. Such internet and web-based banking services are very useful for outstation customers, who have bank accounts with other banks. The following are the reasons, why co-operative banks have to introduce modern banking facilities to their customers.

Not to be obsolete in business or not to be outmoded in banking business, co-operative banks have to introduce and follow modern banking facilities. In the competition, once a banker loses its customer in terms of modern up-to-date banking service, to catch them back will be an uphill task.

Based on the changing business environment and technological developments, co-operative banks have to modernize their banking services.

One of the choices left for a customer to choose a bank is the modernization of banking services and quickness of such banking services. Based on their business experience and their acquaintance with fellow-businessmen, they will choose a banker. A poor performing banker, with outmoded banking services cannot attract such new customers. Better a bank with modern banking facilities, better would be the arrival of new customers and pave way for better customer attraction.

When a bank resorts to modern banking services, naturally the banking business will grow. Existing customers will use this bank and new customers will come under the fold of this bank. Even if the banking charges are slightly higher, customers will not object to it, provided baking services are done quickly applying modern banking systems. To provide modern banking facilities in developing countries, well developed technology is essential. In developed countries, technology would catch quickly.

Banks play a predominant role in uplifting an economy. Whichever economy that has grown fact, the banks would have played a major role. A vibrant banking system promotes investment opportunities. Post-War Japan and Germany's economic miracle was portioned mainly by the banking sector of those countries. Today's economic miracle in China, India and Brazil is due to the brisk banking sector of these countries. Even co-operative banks in these countries have contributed their share of banking development.

8.7 Management Information System (MIS) for Co-operative Banks

Management information system is a device used in modern management circles to provide information needed by the organisations. This information may be relating to the internal and external aspects of the organisation. Information consists of classified and interpreted data that are being used for decision-making. MIS is defined as, "a group of people, a set of manuals and data processing equipment that select, store, process and retrieve data to reduce the uncertainty in decision-making, by yielding information for managers at the time".

8.7.1 Purpose of MIS: The purpose of MIS is, "to raise managing from the level of piecemeal spotty information, intuitive guesswork and isolated problem solving to the level of systems insights, system information, sophisticated data processing and systems problem solving".

The purpose of MIS for co-operative banks has been discussed as follows:

1. Co-operative banks need information to update their services to the customers, as competitive threat is posed by organised commercial banks which use sophisticated computerised information system.
2. To provide efficient and quick services to customers, co-operative banks need to keep all types of data and updated information. Awareness about banking activities among depositors is quite high and co-operative banks cannot provide sub-standard customer service.
3. During the planning stage, co-operative banks need information. Planning a banking programme, planning a deposit mobilisation programme, collection programme etc., warrant to keep lot of information.
4. Decision-making is an important process of co-operative management. To take crucial decisions, the Board must be fed with needed information. The chief executive must provide all information to coordinate their activities.
5. Another management function, coordination needs information. Co-operative banks under a three tier system have to coordinate their activities while issuing loans, collecting deposits, opening branches and collecting loans. Each unit needs information to coordinate their activities.

6. Controlling function of management monitors and measures the implementation of various programmes. To evaluate programmes, classified information is needed.
7. Forecasting is another area of co-operative management which succeeds solely on the information fed. Co-operative banks have to forecast their future in terms of increasing their member customers, deposits, loan operations, crop insurance, loan collections, competitive nature, income, expenditure, etc. These projections will help the co-operative banks to expand their operations in future, to cover more beneficiaries and to improve their efficiency.

8.7.2 Types of Information Needed: Co-operative banks need the following information to be collected from various sources.

1. Systematic information.
2. Non-systematic Information.
3. External Information.
4. Internal Information.
5. Accounting Information.
6. Non-accounting Information.

1. **Systematic Information:** This information is routine information to be collected regularly, say every week, month or quarterly. This information relates to deposits, various types of loans issued, cash flow, collection position etc.
2. **Non-Systematic Information:** Non-systematic information does not have regularity or frequency period. This information is to be collected whenever required. Enough time would be given to collect then needed information. Non-systematic information may be collected either by the staff of the co-operative banks or they can hire outside agencies to collect them. Non-systematic information is of those items when a bank celebrates silver or golden jubilee etc. Public is given all particulars about its growth and development.

3. **External Information:** External Information relates to the banking, economic and related issues. This information is needed to verify the position of the co-operative banks, economic and banking climate that prevails to undertake a new venture like branch banking and whenever co-operatives come under attack from public or legislators to explain their position with facts.
4. **Internal Information:** These are additional information collected in addition of systematic information, including members' behaviour, attitude of the employees and their welfare. This information can be collected on a routine basis or can be collected whenever desired.
5. **Accounting Information:** These are the days of competition and any co-operative institution must be alert to safeguard their interest, members' welfare and employees' welfare. Under such circumstances, monitoring the working of the bank must be a regular feature. Co-operative banks must regularly workout various ratios and keep it ready for comparison. Financial ratios like current ratio, debt equity ratio, profitability ratio etc. must be worked out regularly. Fund flow analysis, cash flow analysis, cash forecasting, working capital management etc. must also be prepared. The stage has come for the staff of co-operative banks to learn modern accounting system and management accounting systems.
6. **Non-accounting Information:** All information other than accounting would be included under this category. It may include external as well as internal information. Deliberations of the Board and general body, minutes of various meetings, official orders and communications received and replies sent etc. can be included under this category.

8.7.3 Agencies Involved to Collect MIS in India: As MIS is getting complex year after year with the use of computers, a single agency in a co-operative banking structure cannot collect all information. Each such activity is costly or it may lead to lot of duplication when many co-operatives of the same nature start collecting banks information independently. Hence, the following agencies can collect information at their own level and such information can be used by all co-operative banks.

1. Primary Agricultural Co-operative Societies (PACS).
2. District Central Co-operative Banks.
3. State Co-operative Banks.
4. District, State and National Co-operatives Unions.
5. Office of the Registrar of Co-operative Societies.
6. NABARD.

1. **Primary Co-operative Banks:** These banks at village level have a direct touch with the agriculturists. They can collect information relating to agricultural economy, agricultural finance and send them to the Central co-operative banks as well as State co-operative banks.
2. **Central Cooperatives Banks:** Central co-operative banks on their part collect information about the economy in the district, performance of various co-operative banks and their own working and problems. Further, they must consolidate the information provided by primary co-operative banks. As members of lead bank scheme, central co-operative banks are fed with lot of additional information. These could be passed on to state co-operative bank and NABARD.
3. **State Co-operative Bank:** A State co-operative bank is the supreme authority on co-operative banking in a state. Having attained this status, they must have all information relating to the co-operative movement, general banking conditions and the economy. They must pass on this information either directly or through published bulletins to all co-operative banks in the state. It has to acquire computers and regularise the information system by way of receiving and sending the needed information. It can have even separate department and establishment for such purposes.

4. **District, State and National Co-operative Unions:** District, state and national co-operative unions are engaged in providing co-operative education to the members of various co-operative units and public. They can equally collect information needed for the co-operative movement. Further, they mobilise public opinion to achieve co-operative goals, consumer awareness programmes, loan collection drives, deposit mobilisation operations, enrolment of new members etc. which are some of the programmes undertaken by co-operative unions. These unions not only collect information on co-operation but also spread the message of co-operation through journals and bulletins published by them. Tamil Nadu Journal of Co-operation, Co-operative News, Co-operator, Indian Journal of Co-operation, Maharashtra Co-operative Quarterly are some of the prominent journals published by various co-operative unions. They provide diverse statistical and non-statistical information.
5. **Office of the Registrar of Co-operative Societies:** In States, the office of the Registrar of Co-operative Societies maintains a separate statistical cell to collect information on various activities of co-operative societies. This information is published in the form of annual reports.
6. **NABARD:** Before the establishment of National Bank for Agriculture and Rural Development (NABARD), collection of information on co-operative movement was undertaken by the Agricultural Credit Department of the RBI. It was also publishing the most valuable statistical statements relating to co-operative movement in India every year. Now this work has been entrusted to the NABARD. This report is published in two volumes—volume I relating to the credit co-operatives and volume II relating to non-credit co-operatives. One of the drawbacks of these reports is that these publications are delayed very much and a time lag of 4 to 5 years exists. To avoid such delay, all State co-operative banks, apex co-operatives and

concerned institutions are expected to send their returns well in advance.

8.8 Role of Co-operative Banks in Green Banking

Green banking means promoting environmental-friendly practices and reducing your carbon footprint from your banking activities. This comes in many forms. Using online banking instead of branch banking; paying bills online instead of mailing them; Opening up CDs and money market accounts at online banks, instead of large multi-branch banks and finding the local bank in your area that is taking the biggest step to support local green initiatives.

Any combination of the above personal banking practices can help the environment. Hence, this leads to the question, which banks are green. In general, online banks and smaller community banks have better track record than larger banks.

For banking professionals, green banking involves the tenets of sustainability, ethical lending, conservation and energy efficiency. Many banks are making dedicated efforts in their local community in these areas. In fact, every week some eco-friendly green banking initiative is announced.

Green banking can benefit the environment either by reducing the carbon footprint of consumers or banks—either works. Either a bank or a consumer can conserve paper and benefit the environment. Ideally, a green banking initiative will involve both. Online banking is an example of this. When a bank's customer goes online, the environmental benefits work both ways. Other examples of what Green Bank Report considers forms of green banking on the consumer side include:

- **Green Checking:** Converting checking accounts to online banking.
- **Green Money Market Accounts:** Converting savings accounts to online banking.
- **Green CDs:** Bonus rates for online banking.
- **Green Loans:** Better rates for energy-efficiency projects.

- **Green Mortgages:** Better rates for energy-efficient houses.
- **Online Bill Payment.**
- **Reward Checking Accounts.**

8.8.1 Green as a Risk Management Approach: Most environmental experts believe that carbon will have a price tag attached to it within the foreseeable future. That price might be in the form of tariffs or it might manifest itself in efficiency incentives. Either way, it gives the finance sector a unique enabling role to play in the transition to a low-carbon economy. Businesses with higher carbon footprints could become higher-risk investments, and banks may begin shifting their focus to financing new technology solutions that capture or reduce carbon emissions.

This presents financial institutions with a new market, including new products for clients in the "Green" segment. For example, services that can help customers identify and manage climate risks—including regulatory, market or physical—or financial solutions to compete in new, green markets. For example, Desjardins the largest financial co-operative group in Canada, designed their energy-efficiency loan product for businesses who want to modernize their equipment and buildings in order to reduce their energy bill and greenhouse gas emissions.

A research initiative by the Presenting Institute and the MIT Green Hub (Cambridge, USA) is designed to better understand how socially responsible green banks operate and to learn how they can have an impact on the society from their work.

The research suggests five levels of socially responsible green banking:

- **Level 1:** Unfocused corporate activities: These include public relations activities that are not part of the core business.
- **Level 2:** Isolated business projects or business practices: Isolated events or products account for a small percentage of a bank's business activity.
- **Level 3:** Systemic business practices: A focus on social

and green objectives is core to the business. The products are designed to achieve social and green objectives.

- **Level 4:** Strategic ecosystem innovation: The engagement does not end at the boundaries of the individual organization but includes the system and environment in which the bank operates.
- **Level 5:** Intentional (purpose-driven) ecosystem innovation: Banks address the core challenges of our time through generative and proactive action and innovation.

8.8.2 Green Banking Initiatives of Bank of Bangladesh: Among the developing countries, Bank of Bangladesh (The Central bank of the country) has taken good efforts towards green banking. Some of the Bank's initiatives are as follows:

1. Environmentally harmful incineration of non re-issuable damaged bank notes is being phased out, resorting instead to shredding.
2. All the departments of Bangladesh Bank's Head Office and its nine branch offices have already been brought under a computer network (LAN/WAN), connecting almost 3,100 PCs.
3. Implementation of Bangladesh Automated Cheque Processing System (BACPS), Bangladesh Electronic Fund Transfer Network (BEFTN), and Enterprise Resources Planning (ERP).
4. Credit Information Bureau online facilities.
5. Enterprise Data Warehouse (EDW) for an electronic data bank.
6. Bangladesh Bank with his network package is now activated on web based e-tendering system.
7. E-recruitment, online salary and other necessary advice, personal file updated information, office orders notification, online balance statements for all members employee of BB, electronic pass for visitors and such many are instantly available.

9

Globalization and Co-operatives

The 1990s witnessed a paradigm shift towards market-oriented economic policies and a careful dismantling of obstacles in its wake. This has helped the smaller, emerging economies gain access to world markets, emergent technologies and collaborations. This has also given them a window to the developed world and helped them understand the significant role of globalization as an instrument, which could be utilised not just to achieve economic efficiency, but also eradicate poverty.

Globalization implies widening and deepening integration with the *globe*, i.e. with people and processes abroad. The trend towards the evolution of a global society is generally thought of in economic terms and in terms of the consequences of the revolution in communication technologies. There is undoubtedly much greater economic integration among the nations of the world today. Globalization is widely seen as the most important factor that could influence economies of nations the world over in the new millennium. The rapid advancement in information technology and communications has made it not just possible but absolutely essential for economies of the world to adapt or fall by the wayside.

9.1 Consequences of Globalization

Globalization has also resulted in the creation of a new business framework. More changes can be expected in the business scenario specifically in terms of openness, adaptiveness and responsiveness. The most important dimensions of economic globalization are: (a) breaking down of national barriers; (b) international spread of trade, financial and production activities, and (c) growing power of transnational corporations and international financial institutions in these processes. While economic globalization is a very uneven process, with increased trade and investment being focused in a few countries, almost all countries are greatly affected by this process.

A major consequence of globalization is the growing concentration and monopolisation of economic resources and power by transnational corporations and by global financial firms and funds. This process has been termed transnationalisation, in which fewer and fewer transnational corporations are gaining a large and rapidly increasing proportion of world economic resources, production and market shares. Where a multinational company used to dominate the market of a single product, a big transnational company (TNC) now typically produces or trades in an increasing multitude of products, services and sectors. Through mergers and acquisitions, fewer and fewer of these TNCs now control a larger and larger share of the global market, whether in commodities, manufactures or services.

Another consequence of globalization is the internationalization of national policies and policy-making mechanism. National policies (including economic, social, cultural and technological) that until recently were determined by the States and people within a country have increasingly come under the influence of international agencies and processes or by big private corporations and economic/ financial players. This has led to the narrowed ability of governments and people to make choices from options in economic, social and cultural policies.

Most developing countries have seen their independent policy-making mechanism capacity eroded, and have to adopt policies influenced by other entities, which may on balance be detrimental to the countries concerned. The developed countries, where the major economic players reside, and which also control the processes and policies of international economic agencies, are better able to maintain control over their own national policies as well as determine the policies and practices of international institutions and the global system. However, it is also true that the large corporations have taken over a large part of decision-making even in the developed countries, at the expense of the power of the state or political and social leaders.

9.2 Globalization and Developing Countries

The issue that concerns developing countries is how one can ensure greater participation of the weaker economies in the global process and what needs to be done to ensure that the course of globalization benefits more people in more countries. The uneven and unequal nature of the present globalization is manifested in the fast growing gap between the rich and poor people of the world and between developed and developing countries; and by the large differences among nations in the distribution of gains and losses.

This imbalance leads to polarisation between countries and groups that gain, and the many countries and groups in society that lose out or are marginalised. Globalization, polarisation, wealth concentration and marginalisation are therefore linked through the same process. In this process, investment resources, growth and modern technology are focused on a few countries, mainly in North America, Europe, Japan and a few East Asian countries. A majority of developing countries are excluded from the process, or are participating in it in marginal ways.

Although the developed world is in a dominant position and has been prepared to use this to further their control of the global economy, the developing countries have not done well in organising themselves to co-ordinate on substantial policy and negotiating positions. The developed countries, on the other hand, are well-organised within their own countries, with well-staffed departments dealing with international trade and finance, and with university academics and private and quasi government think tanks helping to obtain information and map policies and strategies. They also have well-organised associations and lobbies associated with their corporations and financial institutions, which have great influence over the government departments.

On the positive side, globalization has compelled developing countries to improve overall economic management, and make their economies efficient. To get a share of global capital and technology, developing countries have to upgrade their social and economic institutions through administrative, legislative and legal reforms. The quality of governance has to improve to encourage productivity and efficiency. Political stability has to be established. In this context, following lessons can be drawn from East Asian countries:

1. Developing human capital is a basic pre-requisite. Successful globalization and the knowledge economy require educated, healthy and skilled people.
2. It is necessary to build up domestic savings and put them to productive use.
3. Sound economic management and macro-economic balances are necessary. Large fiscal deficit is a serious obstacle to globalization.
4. Good governance at the national and sub-national levels builds confidence among investors.
5. Transparency has to be established in the functioning of both government and business units.
6. Free and open market economies require effective regulatory authorities because role of government changes from control and regulation to governance and facilitation.
7. Modernised capital markets with effective regulatory authorities are necessary to impart confidence to investors by maintaining stability and regulating speculative forces.

9.3 Adverse Effects of Globalization on Women

With the growing globalization and liberalization of the economy as well as increased privatization of services, women as a whole have been left behind and not been able to partake of the fruits of success. Mainstreaming of women into the new and emerging areas of growth is imperative. This will require training and skill upgradation in emerging trades, encouraging more women to take up vocational training and employment in the boom sectors. This will also require women to migrate to cities and metros for work. Provision of safe housing, and other gender friendly facilities at work will need to be provided.

Another facet of globalization is related to the fact that many persons especially women will be severely affected with the advent of setting up of industrial parks, national highways, special economic zones (SEZs) etc. as huge tracts of farm land are likely to be acquired for this purpose. This would require massive resettlement of the displaced persons and their families. It is, therefore, essential that a viable resettlement policy and strategy is formulated and put in place immediately which clearly reflects the needs of women impacted by globalization/displacement.

With the removal of all quantitative restrictions on the import of various products, the self-employed women's groups, especially in the informal sector, have started facing competition from the low-priced imported consumer goods which are invading the Indian market. Although this has the imminent danger of displacing a large number of employed/self-employed women, but at the same time, the process of globalization has also opened up opportunities for women entrepreneurs for exporting their products to the markets all over the world. Globalization has thus opened up new challenges for the realization of thc goal of women's empowerment. Hence, strategies should be designed to enhance the capacity of women and empower them to cope with the negative economic and social impacts of the globalization process.

Several studies have indicated that adverse consequences of globalization are disproportionately borne by women.

Increased mechanization leading to displacement of female unskilled workers, increased migration of male workers in traditionally women-dominated areas, increase in female-headed household due to migration of males are some of the trends established in various studies.

Globalization has presented new challenges for the realization of the goal of women's equality, the gender impact of which has not been systematically evaluated fully. However, it is evident that there is a need for re-framing policies for access to employment and equality of employment. Benefits of the growing global economy have been unevenly distributed leading to wider economic disparities, the feminization of poverty, increased gender inequality through deteriorating working conditions and unsafe working environment especially in the informal economy and rural areas. Strategies need to be designed to enhance the capacity of women and empower them to meet the negative social and economic impacts, which may flow from the globalization process.

With upgradation of skills, opportunities for employment of women exist in several areas such as health services, food processing and crafts. Key areas of concern include women in small subsistence farming households, women workers in garment and textiles who will face increased competition after the phasing out of the Multi Fibre Agreement in 2005, and women displaced by new technologies in sectors such as construction, which have traditionally absorbed large numbers of women.

With the onset of trade liberalisation, women in India today are linked to the global economy to a very significant extent, as producers, entrepreneurs, service providers, consumers and citizens. There is a need to identify capacity constraints and entry barriers that prevent women from securing gains from trade. Trade-related awareness and capacity building of the women stakeholders need to be prioritised.

The globalization process has, in some countries, resulted in policy shifts in favour of more open trade and financial flows, privatization of state-owned enterprises and in many cases lower public spending particularly on social services. This change has transformed patterns of production and accelerated technological advances in information and communication and affected the lives of women, both as workers and consumers. In a large number of countries, particularly in developing and least developed countries, these changes have also adversely impacted on the lives of women and have increased inequality. The gender impact of these changes has not been systematically evaluated. Globalization has also affected cultural values, lifestyles and forms of communication.

In countries with economies in transition women are bearing most of the hardships induced by the economic restructuring and being the first to lose jobs in times of recession. They are being squeezed out from fast growth sectors. Loss of childcare facilities due to elimination or privatization of state work places, increased need for older care without the corresponding facilities, continuing inequality of access to training for finding re-employment and to productive assets for entering or expanding businesses are current challenges facing women in these countries.

9.4 Opportunities Offered by Globalization

Science and technology, as fundamental components of development, are transforming patterns of production, contributing to the creation of jobs and new job classifications, and ways of working, and contributing to the establishment of a knowledge-based society. Technological change can bring new opportunities for all women in all fields if they have equal access, and adequate training. Women should also be actively involved in the definition, design, development, implementation and gender impact evaluation of policies related to these changes. Many women world-wide are yet to effectively use these new communications technologies for networking, advocacy, exchange of information business, education, media consultation and e-commerce initiatives. For instance, millions of the world's poorest women and men still do not have access to and benefits from science and technology and are currently excluded from this new field and the opportunities it presents.

The patterns of migratory flows of labour are changing. Women and girls are increasingly involved in internal, regional and international labour migration to pursue many occupations mainly in farm labour, domestic work and some forms of entertainment work. While this situation increases their earning opportunities and self-reliance, it also exposes them—particularly the poor, uneducated, unskilled and/or undocumented migrants—to inadequate working conditions, increased health risk, the risk of trafficking, economic and sexual exploitation, racism, racial discrimination and xenophobia, and other forms of abuse.

Further, globalization has dramatically changed the conditions under which the work for gender equality must be carried out, especially in high growth countries like India. While globalization has generated opportunities for local producers and entrepreneurs to reach international markets, it has at times intensified existing inequalities and insecurities for many poor women. Since the gains of globalization are often concentrated in the hands of those with higher education—those who own resources and have access to capital—poor women are usually the least able to seize the longer term opportunities offered.

This disadvantage has been exacerbated as in most of the countries, policies reflect a commitment to global norms of markets and social policy is increasingly determined by market dynamics. Market-friendly policies generate high growth rates that fail to translate into improved standards of health, education and human security. Feminist scholars have highlighted the gendered impact of such policies, many of which increase women's job vulnerability, unpaid work burden, while reducing state level resources that might be used to provide a social safety net.

Owing to dissent voiced by feminist scholars on the widespread assumption that gender inequality as a challenge can be overcome with effective and sustained advocacy as it is more about mindsets and less about policies, especially economic policies, there have been some attempts to integrate economic and social policies but gender concerns have not been accorded requisite attention. These disadvantages have led to a situation where gains in women's economic opportunities lag behind those in women's capabilities.

9.5 Role of Co-operatives in the Globalized World

Co-operatives are one of primarily, autonomous, economic institutions of user members united voluntarily to meet their common economic, social, cultural needs and aspirations through a jointly-owned and democratically-controlled enterprise. They are self-reliant and self-sustaining institutions functioning in a free, fair and transparent way in keeping with the principles and values of the co-operative movement. To arrest the practice of concentration of power in a few hands to the detriment of the larger member community, education for awareness building should be an integral part of a co-operative.

Agro-processing of fruits and vegetables is a potential area for development of co-operatives of the farmers. These processing units should, ideally, be part of integrated projects linking production with agro-processing and supporting by products. The major weaknesses of the co-operative fruit and vegetable processing units are under-utilisation of capacity and inefficient technical and financial management.

The recent changes introduced by the Government in several fields provide an opportunity for co-operatives to play a much larger role in several areas such as marketing of agricultural produce, creation of marketing infrastructure, establishment of agro-processing units etc.

Co-operatives in India being a State subject have been and continue to be variously governed through multiple individual State Acts. The Acts endow governments with draconian powers which have in many cases militated against the very concept of a co-operative. Supersession of elected boards of co-operatives and appointment of special officers for long periods without elections are examples of the interference of state governments in co-operative functioning.

The global economy, and in particular the Indian economy, is passing through transformation. The positive dimension of globalization includes liberal economic policies, reduction of state intervention, and easy access to monetary capital and consequently new opportunities for economic participation. This is already evidenced in India in the form of increased economic growth and state withdrawal from many economic and social domains. On the other hand, there is apparently a misplaced perception developing in India that co-operatives may not be able to deliver in the context of the globalized market conditions and the changes that are taking place as a result.

Under the circumstances, there is a need for resurgence of co-operatives as important players. Co-operatives have tremendous opportunities because: (a) they have a special identity, (b) they have both social and economic objectives, (c) they are value- and community-based, (d) they are people-oriented, and (e) they have a network of linkages through the co-operative movement.

In terms of the decent work paradigm, co-operatives could lead the way by demonstrating what is really meant by freedom, equity, security and human dignity. Thus, co-operatives by being true to their basic principles provide locally-based answers to globalization. Therefore, contrary to the belief that globalization impedes the growth of co-operatives, they are the vital agencies to face the challenges posed by globalization.

Co-operatives in India have mostly played the role of an agent of the government. Co-operatives are seen to be the institutions that carry the State programmes to people, and in turn get State support.

9.5.1 Occupying New Spaces: Globalization and liberalization of economic policies creates new spaces in two forms. First, the governments are withdrawing from different domains hitherto solely or generally occupied by them creating vacant spaces, be it in manufacturing or service sector. Secondly, additional opportunities are continuously being created in newer areas, under the new economic environment. Many of these domains are not regarded as being commercially attractive. However, they are very important for people and communities and there is definitely a demand for these services. As such, the challenge would be to make them commercially viable and profitable. Traditional areas of social sector such as education, health, transportation, water supply, forest management, electricity are some of the areas where co-operative solutions could be superior to either public or private approaches to utility management. In fact, privatization efforts in India are already on in this area. Co-operatives have been working in all these areas and have the potential to prove their strength and hence they could be effective alternatives to privatization.

Further, co-operatives could play a major role in newer areas such as precision farming, sun farming, water harvesting, micro finance. Other potential areas are information technology, communications, tourism and hospitality etc., the demand for which is ever growing and which could provide alternative means of livelihood for co-operative members. Outsourcing of services would also be the practice as firms grow in size and specialization. Such outsourcing would expectedly lead to savings in transaction costs. Entering such services through the co-operative route could prove an attractive alternative employment generating avenue.

9.5.2 Providing an Institutional Form for the Displaced: Globalization would also result in restructuring leading to displacements occurring due to exit policies, labour re-engineering, closure of less competitive units, adoption of new technologies and consequent down sizing, mergers, acquisitions etc. including displacement from the agricultural sector. Displaced specialists could form co-operatives for providing essential specialized services, which institutions would be increasingly outsourcing. There has been a sharp reduction in the population dependent on agriculture and landless labourers have increased in number. The alarming rate of unemployment among youth continues. Collective endeavours through co-operatives of such marginalized sections of the people can work, as many services would still be required by existing concerns which may not wish to have such service providers on their pay roll.

9.5.3 Constructive Competitors: Cartels or pre-determined market sharing by private enterprises can jeopardize free and fair trade. Co-operatives could provide the role of the constructive competitors. This could be either through a stand-alone co-operative or by entering strategic partnership with the private sector in the form of co-operative-private sector collaborations etc. Co-operatives by their very presence would help to maintain the balance in terms of price and quality. For this reason, co-operatives need to enter all those areas where full domination by the private corporate might eventually spell bad news to the consumers.

9.5.4 Safeguarding the Interest of Agriculture and Rural Areas: Agriculture will continue to be very important in terms of percentage share of dependent population. The logic of agriculture would be applicable to almost the entire rural population. Self-help initiatives by farmers in the area of cultivation, marketing, accessing agricultural inputs, finding jobs for the landless labourers, displaced rural artisans etc., would continue to be a major role for the co-operative sector. None else is equipped to handle this.

9.5.5 Facilitating the Millennium Development Goals (MDGs): The Government of India has its commitment to the UN, of achieving the MDGs within a specified time frame. In many of the specified areas, the country is clearly lagging behind. Rural health (and in particular maternal health) and combating contagious diseases (medical co-operatives), gender equity (women co-operatives), and poverty reduction (agricultural and tribal co-operatives) are some of the crucial areas under MDGs, where the co-operative sector can play the lead role.

9.5.6 Preserving the Cultural and Ethical Values of the Country: Co-operatives are the best channels to keep the spirit of collectivism and democracy afloat. The presence of a large network of social organizations, like co-operatives, would aid in the generation and utilization of social capital and more the social capital, greater would be the possibility of development. Therefore, co-operatives have a futuristic role of fostering collectivism and preserving the social capital base of the country.

It is thus clear that co-operatives have a significant role to play in the future settings of the Indian economy. In fact they have a more important role to play in the future compared to their agency role of the past. It is only the presence of a strong and wide network of co-operatives that can make the process of globalization less painful and global integration smooth. It is the co-operatives again who are equipped to work as pressure groups to voice views of the people in the market.

To sum up, socio-economically disadvantaged are yet to benefit from globalization. The challenge to overcome the scourge of poverty remains a daunting task. The support of the poor for reforms and their involvement in the development process can be achieved only if they start benefiting from government policies. It is necessary to ensure that the poor and the deprived have a greater stake in economic reforms than at present for mobilising their enthusiastic participation in the development process. Economic reforms must be guided by compassion and distributive justice. Improvement of living conditions of the poorest and the weakest sections of society should be high priority areas of welfare and development programmes/schemes of the government.

Globalization is an irreversible trend and developing economies are also inevitably involved in the process. Developed countries should, therefore, carefully consider how to restructure the world trading system to accommodate developing economies, by enabling them to benefit from Globalization while minimising external shocks. The World Trade Organization (WTO) should work more effectively, through an enlargement of waiver clauses which recognise the weaker position of developing countries.

Despite distortions and aberrations, Globalization is a reality. Developments in information and communication technologies are unifying markets and people, cutting across barriers of space and time. At the end of the day, one has to understand and accept that globalization is the stratagem for the new millennium. Every country, developed and developing, has to accept this and formulate their economies around it.

Glossary of Banking Terms

Glossary of Banking Terms

A

Account Agreement: The contract governing your open-end credit account, it provides information on changes that may occur to the account.

Account History: The payment history of an account over a specific period of time, including the number of times the account was past due or over limit.

Account Holder: Any and all persons designated and authorized to transact business on behalf of an account. Each account holder's signature needs to be on file with the bank. The signature authorizes that person to conduct business on behalf of the account.

Accrued Interest: Interest that has been earned but not yet paid.

Acquiring Bank: In a merger, the bank that absorbs the bank acquired.

Adjustable-Rate Mortgages (ARMS): Also known as variable-rate mortgages. The initial interest rate is usually below that of conventional fixed-rate loans. The interest rate may change over the life of the loan as market conditions change. There is typically a maximum (or ceiling) and a minimum (or floor) defined in the loan agreement. If interest rates rise, so does the loan payment. If interest rates fall, the loan payment may as well.

Adverse Action: Under the Equal Credit Opportunity Act, a creditor's refusal to grant credit on the terms requested, termination of an existing account, or an unfavourable change in an existing account.

Adverse Action Notice: The notice required by the Equal Credit Opportunity Act advising a credit applicant or existing debtor of the denial of their request for credit or advising of a change in terms considered unfavourable to the account holder.

Affidavit: A sworn statement in writing before a proper official, such as a notary public.

Alteration: Any change involving an erasure or rewriting in the date, amount, or payee of a cheque or other negotiable instrument.

Amortization: The process of reducing debt through regular instalment payments of principal and interest that will result in the payoff of a loan at its maturity.

Annual Percentage Rate (APR): The cost of credit on a yearly basis, expressed as a percentage.

Annual Percentage Yield (APY): A percentage rate reflecting the total amount of interest paid on a deposit account based on the interest rate and the frequency of compounding for a 365-day year.

Annuity: A life insurance contract sold by insurance companies, brokers, and other financial institutions. It is usually sold as a retirement investment. An annuity is a long-term investment and can have steep surrender charges and penalties for withdrawal before the annuity's maturity date.

Application: Under the Equal Credit Opportunity Act (ECOA), an oral or written request for an extension of credit that is made in accordance with the procedures established by a creditor for the type of credit requested.

Appraisal: The act of evaluating and setting the value of a specific piece of personal or real property.

Authorization: The issuance of approval, by a credit card issuer, merchant, or other affiliate, to complete a credit card transaction.

Automated Clearing House (ACH): A computerized facility used by member depository institutions to electronically combine, sort, and distribute inter-bank credits and debits. ACHs process electronic transfers of government securities and provided customer services, such as direct deposit of customers' salaries and government benefit payments (i.e., social security, welfare, and veterans' entitlements), and preauthorized transfers.

Automated Teller Machine (ATM): A machine, activated by a magnetically encoded card or other medium that can process a variety of banking transactions. These include accepting deposits and loan payments, providing withdrawals, and transferring funds between accounts.

Automatic Bill Payment: A cheque less system for paying recurring bills with one authorization statement to a financial institution. For example, the customer would only have to provide one authorization form/letter/document to pay the cable bill each month. The necessary debits and credits are made through an automated clearing house (ACH).

Availability Date: Bank's policy as to when funds deposited into an account will be available for withdrawal.

Availability Policy: Bank's policy as to when funds deposited into an account will be available for withdrawal.

Available Balance: The balance of an account less any hold, uncollected funds, and restrictions against the account.

Available Credit: The difference between the credit limit assigned to a cardholder account and the present balance of the account.

B

Balance Transfer: The process of moving an outstanding balance from one credit card to another. This is usually done to obtain a lower interest rate on the outstanding balance. Transfers are sometimes subjected to a balance transfer fee.

Bank Custodian: A bank custodian is responsible for maintaining the safety of clients' assets held at one of the custodian's premises, a sub-custodian facility or an outside depository.

Bank Examination: Examination of a bank's assets, income, and expenses, as well as operations by representatives of Federal and State bank supervisory authority, to ensure that the bank is solvent and is operating in conformity with banking laws and sound banking principles.

Bank Statement: Periodically the bank provides a statement of a customer's deposit account. It shows all deposits made, all cheques paid, and other debits posted during the period (usually one month), as well as the current balance.

Banking Day: A business day during which an office of a bank is open to the public for substantially all of its banking functions.

Bankrupt: A bankrupt person, firm, or corporation has insufficient assets to cover their debts. The debtor seeks relief through a court proceeding to work out a payment schedule or erase debts. In some cases, the debtor must surrender control of all assets to a court-appointed trustee.

Bankruptcy: The legal proceedings by which the affairs of a bankrupt person are turned over to a trustee or receiver for administration under the bankruptcy laws. There are two types of bankruptcy: (i) Involuntary bankruptcy—one or more creditors of an insolvent debtor file a petition having the debtor declared bankrupt, and (ii) Voluntary bankruptcy—the debtor files a petition claiming inability to meet financial obligations and willingness to be declared bankrupt.

Beneficiary: A person who is entitled to receive the benefits or proceeds of a will, trust, insurance policy, retirement plan, annuity, or other contract.

Billing Cycle: The time interval between the dates on which regular periodic statements are issued.

Billing Date: The month, date, and year when a periodic or monthly statement is generated. Calculations have been performed for appropriate finance charges, minimum payment due, and new balance.

Billing Error: A charge that appears on a periodic statement associated with an extension of credit (e.g., credit card) that: (a) was not authorized by the cardholder or the cardholders' designee, (b) is not properly identified, and (c) was not accepted by the cardholder or the cardholder's designee.

A billing error can also be caused by a creditor's failure to credit a payment or other credit to an account as well as accounting and clerical errors.

Business Day: Any day on which offices of a bank are open to the public for carrying on substantially all of the bank's business.

C

Cancelled Cheque: A cheque that a bank has paid, charged to the account holder's account, and then endorsed. Once cancelled, a cheque is no longer negotiable.

Cashier's Cheque: A cheque drawn on the funds of the bank, not against the funds in a depositor's account. However, the depositor paid for the cashier's cheque with funds from their account. The primary benefit of a cashier's cheque is that the recipient of the cheque is assured that the funds are available.

Cease and Desist Letter: A letter requesting that a company stops the activity mentioned in the letter.

Certificate of Deposit: A negotiable instrument issued by a bank in exchange for funds, usually bearing interest, deposited with the bank.

Certificate of Release: A certificate signed by a lender indicating that a mortgage has been fully paid and all debts satisfied.

Certified Cheque: A personal cheque drawn by an individual that is certified (guaranteed) to be good. The face of the cheque bears the words "certified" or "accepted", and is signed by an official of the bank or thrift institution issuing the cheque. The signature signifies that: (a) the signature of the drawer is genuine, and (b) sufficient funds are on deposit and earmarked for payment of the cheque.

Charge-off: The balance on a credit obligation that a lender no longer expects to be repaid and writes off as a bad debt.

Cheque: A written order instructing a financial institution to pay immediately on demand a specified amount of money from the cheque writer's account to the person named on the cheque or, if a specific person is not named, to whoever bears the cheque to the institution for payment.

Cheque Truncation: The conversion of data on a cheque into an electronic image after a cheque enters the processing system. Cheque truncation eliminates the need to return cancelled cheques to customers.

Cheque Account: A demand deposit account subject to withdrawal of funds by cheque.

Closed-End Credit: Generally, any credit sale agreement in which the amount advanced, plus any finance charges, is expected to be repaid in full by a specified date. Most real estate and automobile loans are closed-end agreements.

Closed-End Loan: Generally, any loan in which the amount advanced, plus any finance charges, is expected to be repaid in full by a specified date. Most real estate and automobile loans are closed-end agreements.

Closing a Mortgage Loan: The consummation of a contractual real estate transaction in which all appropriate documents are signed and the proceeds of the mortgage loan are then disbursed by the lender.

Closing Costs: The expenses incurred by sellers and buyers in transferring ownership in real property. The costs of closing may include the origination fee, discount points, attorneys' fees, loan fees, title search and insurance, survey charge, recordation fees, and the credit report charge.

Collateral: Assets that are offered to secure a loan or other credit. For example, if you get a real estate mortgage, the bank's collateral is typically your house. Collateral becomes subject to seizure on default.

Collected Funds: Cash deposits or cheques that have been presented for payment and for which payment has been received.

Collection Agency: A company hired by a creditor to collect a debt that is owed. Creditors typically hire a collection agency only after they have made efforts to collect the debt themselves, usually through letters and telephone calls.

Collection Items: Items-such as drafts, notes, and acceptances-received for collection and credited to a depositor's account after payment has been received. Collection items are usually subject to special instructions and may involve additional fees. Most banks impose a special fee, called a collection charge, for handling collection items.

Co-maker: A person who signs a note to guarantee a loan made to another person and is jointly liable with the maker for repayment of the loan (also known as a co-signer).

Consumer Credit Counselling Service: A service which specializes in working with consumers who are overextended with debts and need to make arrangements with creditors.

Consumer Reporting Agency: An agency that regularly collects or evaluates individual consumer credit information or other information about consumers and sells consumer reports for a fee to creditors or others. Typical clients include banks, mortgage lenders, credit card companies, and other financing companies.

Conventional Fixed Rate Mortgage: A fixed-rate mortgage offers you a set interest rate and payments that do not change throughout the life, or "term", of the loan. A conventional fixed-rate loan is fully paid off over a given number of years-usually 15, 20, or 30. A portion of each monthly payment goes towards paying back the money borrowed, the “principal”; the rest is “interest”.

Co-Signer: An individual who signs the note of another person as support for the credit of the primary signer and who becomes responsible for the obligation (also known as a Co-maker).

Credit Application: A form to be completed by an applicant for a credit account, giving sufficient details (residence, employment, income, and existing debt) to allow the seller to establish the applicant's creditworthiness. Sometimes, an application fee is charged to cover the cost of loan processing.

Credit Card Account Agreement: A written agreement that explains the: (a) terms and conditions of the account, (b) credit usage and payment by the cardholder, and (c) duties and responsibilities of the card issuer.

Credit Card Issuer: Any financial institution that issues bank cards to those who apply for them.

Credit Disability Insurance: A type of insurance, also known as accident and health insurance that makes payments on the loan if you become ill or injured and cannot work.

Credit Life Insurance: A type of life insurance that helps repay a loan if you should die before the loan is fully repaid. This is optional coverage.

Credit Limit: The maximum amount of credit that is available on a credit card or other line of credit account.

Credit Repair Organization: A person or organization that sells, provides, performs, or assists in improving a consumer's credit record, credit history or credit rating (or says that that they will do so) in exchange for a fee or other payment. It also includes a person or organization that provides advice or assistance about how to improve a consumer's credit record, credit history or credit rating. There are some important exceptions to this definition, including many non-profit organizations and the creditor that is owed the debt.

Credit Report: A detailed report of an individual's credit history prepared by a credit bureau and used by a lender in determining a loan applicant's creditworthiness.

Credit Score: A number, roughly between 300 and 800, that measures an individual's credit worthiness. The most well-known type of credit score is the FICO® score. This score represents the answer from a mathematical formula that assigns numerical values to various pieces of information in your credit report. Banks use a credit score to help determine whether you qualify for a particular credit card, loan, or service.

Cut-Off Time: A time of day established by a bank for receipt of deposits. After the cut-off time, deposits are considered received on the next banking day.

D

Debit: A debit may be an account entry representing money you owe a lender or money that has been taken from your deposit account.

Debit Card: A debit card allows the account owner to access their funds electronically. Debit cards may be used to obtain cash from automated teller machines or purchase goods or services using point-of-sale systems. The use of a debit card involves immediate debiting and crediting of consumers' accounts.

Debt Collector: Any person who regularly collects debts owed to others.

Debt Elimination Scheme: A debt elimination scheme is a plan that is advertised as a way for an individual to eliminate various types of debt simply by paying someone a small fee compared to the amount of debt to be eliminated. These schemes are fraudulent. As a result of using a fraudulent scheme, individuals will lose money, could lose property, will damage their credit rating, and possibly incur additional debt. In addition, a creditor may take legal action against an individual to resolve a fraudulent attempt to eliminate debt. It is also possible for the victim to have identify theft occur by participating in such a fraudulent scheme.

Debtor: Someone who owes monies to another party.

Debt-to-Income Ratio (DTI): The percentage of a consumer's monthly gross income that goes toward paying debts. Generally, the higher the ratio, the higher the perceived risk. Loans with higher risk are generally priced at a higher interest rate.

Decedent: A deceased person, ordinarily used with respect to one who has died recently.

Deferred Payment: A payment postponed until a future date.

Delinquency: A debt that was not paid when due.

Demand Deposit: A deposit of funds that can be withdrawn without any advance notice.

Deposit Slip: An itemized memorandum of the cash and other funds that a customer presents to the bank for credit to his or her account.

Derogatory Information: Data received by a creditor indicating that a credit applicant has not paid his or her accounts with other creditors according to the required terms.

Direct Deposit: A payment that is electronically deposited into an individual's account at a depository institution.

Direct Dispute: A dispute submitted directly to the furnisher about the accuracy of information in your consumer report that relates to an account or other relationship you have with the furnisher.

Disclosures: Certain information that Federal and State laws require creditors to give to borrowers relative to the terms of the credit extended.

Draft: A signed, written order by which one party (the drawer) instructs another party (the drawee) to pay a specified sum to a third party (the payee), at sight or at a specific date. Typical bank drafts are negotiable instruments and are similar in many ways to cheques.

Drawee: The person (or bank) who is expected to pay a cheque or draft when it is presented for payment.

Drawee Bank: The bank upon which a cheque is drawn.

Drawer: The person who writes a cheque or draft instructing the drawee to pay someone else.

E

Electronic Banking: A service that allows an account holder to obtain account information and manage certain banking transactions through a personal computer via the financial institution's Web site on the Internet (This is also known as Internet or online banking).

Electronic Cheque Conversion: Electronic cheque conversion is a process in which your cheque is used as a source of information-for the cheque number, your account number, and the number that identifies your financial institution. The information is then used to make a one-time electronic payment from your account-an electronic fund transfer. The cheque itself is not the method of payment.

Electronic Funds Transfer (EFT): The transfer of money between accounts by consumer electronic systems-such as automated teller machines (ATMs) and electronic payment of bills-rather than by cheque or cash (wire transfers, cheques, drafts, and paper instruments do not fall into this category).

Embezzlement: In most States, embezzlement is defined as theft/larceny of assets (money or property) by a person in a position of trust or responsibility over those assets. Embezzlement typically occurs in the employment and corporate settings.

Encoding: The process used to imprint or inscribe MICR characters on cheques, deposits, and other financial instruments. [Magnetic Ink Character Recognition (MICR) is a character-recognition technology adopted mainly by the banking industry to facilitate the processing of cheques. Each chéque in encoded at the bottom with the dollar amount of the cheque. If that information is entered incorrectly, there is an encoding error.]

Equal Credit Opportunity Act (ECOA): Prohibits creditors from discriminating against credit applicants on the basis of race, colour, religion, national origin, sex, marital status, age, or because an applicant receives income from a public assistance program.

Error Resolution: The required process for resolving errors involving electronic transfers to and from deposit accounts.

Escheat: Reversion of real or personal property to the State when (i) a person dies without leaving a will and has no heirs, or (ii) when the property (such as a bank account) has been inactive for a certain period of time.

Escrow: A financial instrument held by a third party on behalf of the other two parties in a transaction. The funds are held by the escrow service until it receives the appropriate written or oral instructions—or until obligations have been fulfilled. Securities, funds, and other assets can be held in escrow.

Escrow Analysis: The periodic examination of escrow accounts by a mortgage company to verify that monthly deposits are sufficient to pay taxes, insurance, and other escrow-related items on when due.

Escrow Funds: Funds held in reserve by a mortgage company to pay taxes, insurance, and other mortgage-related items when due.

Estate Account: An account held in the name of a decedent that is administered by an executor or administrator of the estate.

Exception Hold: A period of time that allows the banks to exceed the maximum hold periods defined in the Expedited

Funds Availability Act.

F

Fiduciary: Undertaking to act as executor, administrator, guardian, conservator, or trustee for a family trust, authorized trust, or testamentary trust, or receiver or trustee in bankruptcy.

Finance Charge: The total cost of credit a customer must pay on a consumer loan, including interest. The Truth in Lending Act requires disclosure of the finance charge.

Financial Regulatory Agency: An organization authorized by statute for ensuring the safe and sound operation of financial institutions chartered to conduct business under that agency's jurisdiction.

First Mortgage: A real estate loan which is in a first lien position, taking priority over all other liens. In case of a foreclosure, the first mortgage will be repaid before any other mortgages.

Fixed Rate Loan: The interest rate and the payment remain the same over the life of the loan. The consumer makes equal monthly payments of principal and interest until the debt is paid in full.

Fixed Rate Mortgage: A mortgage with payments that remain the same throughout the life of the loan because the interest rate and other terms are fixed and do not change.

Float: (a) The amount of uncollected funds represented by cheques in the possession of one bank but drawn on other banks; (b) The time that elapses between the day a cheque is deposited and the day it is presented for payment to the financial institution on which it is drawn.

Flood Insurance: Flood insurance protects against water from an overflowing river or a hurricane's tidal surge and also covers damage from water that builds up during storms.

Flood Plain: A strip of relatively flat and normally dry land alongside a stream, river, or lake that is covered by water during a flood.

Foreclosure: A legal process in which property that is collateral or security for a loan may be sold to help repay the loan when the loan is in default.

Foreign Transaction Fees: A fee assessed by your bank for making a transaction at another bank's ATM.

Forged Cheque: A cheque on which the drawer's signature has been forged.

Forgery: The fraudulent signing or alteration of another's name to an instrument such as a deed, mortgage, or cheque. The intent of the forgery is to deceive or defraud.

Fraud Alert: A key provision of the Fair and Accurate Credit Transactions Act of 2003 is the consumer's ability to place a fraud alert on their credit record. A consumer would use this option if they believe they were a victim of identity theft.

The alert requires any creditor that is asked to extend credit to contact the consumer by phone and verify that the credit application was not made by an identity thief.

Frozen Account: An account on which funds may not be withdrawn until a lien is satisfied and a court order or other legal process makes the account available for withdrawal (e.g., the account of a deceased person is frozen pending a court order distributing the funds to the new lawful owners).

An account may also be frozen when there is a dispute regarding the true ownership of an account. The bank will freeze the account to preserve the existing funds until legal action can determine the lawful owner.

Furnisher: An entity that provides information about a consumer to a consumer reporting agency for inclusion in a consumer report.

G

Garnishment/Garnish: A legal process that allows a creditor to remove funds from your bank account to satisfy a debt that you have not paid. If you owe money to a person or company, they can obtain a court order directing your bank to take money out of your account to pay off your debt.

Guaranteed Student Loan: An extension of credit from a financial institution that is guaranteed by a Federal or State government entity to assist with tuition and other educational expenses. The government entity is responsible for paying the interest on the loan and paying the lender to manage it. The government entity also is responsible for the loan if the student defaults.

Guarantor: A party who agrees to be responsible for the payment of another party's debts should that party default.

H

Hold: Used to indicate that a certain amount of a customer's balance may not be withdrawn until an item has been collected, or until a specific cheque or debit is posted.

Home Equity Line of Credit (HELOC): A line of credit secured by the equity in a consumer's home. It can be used for home improvements, debt consolidation, and other major purchases. Interest paid on the loan is generally tax deductible (consult a tax advisor to be sure). The funds may be accessed by writing cheques against the line of credit or by getting a cash advance.

Home Equity Loan: A home equity loan allows you to tap into your home's built-up equity, which is the difference between the amount that your home could be sold for and the amount that you still owe. Homeowners often use a home-equity loan for home improvements, to pay for a new car, or to finance their child's college education. The interest paid is usually tax-deductible. Because the loan is secured by your home's equity, if you default, the bank may foreclose on your house and take ownership of it. This type of loan is sometimes referred to as a second mortgage or borrowing against your home.

I

Inactive Account: An account that has little or no activity; neither deposits nor withdrawals having been posted to the account for a significant period of time.

Index-linked Certificate of Deposit: An index-linked CD is a deposit obligation of the issuing bank and is often sold through bank branches and affiliated and unaffiliated brokers. Index-linked CDs provide the investor the ability to participate in the appreciation, if any, of a particular index, during the term of the CD. Index-linked CDs may have complicated payout structures and may not be suitable or appropriate for all investors. Investors should carefully review the investment risk considerations detailed in the relevant offering documents and disclosure statements. Index-linked CDs are not securities and are not registered under securities laws.

Individual Account: An account in the name of one individual.

Individual Retirement Account (IRA): A retirement savings programme for individuals to which yearly tax-deductible contributions up to a specified limit can be made. The amount contributed is not taxed until withdrawn. Withdrawal is not permitted without penalty until the individual reaches a specified age.

Insufficient Funds: When a depositor's cheque account balance is inadequate to pay a cheque presented for payment.

Insurance (Hazard): Insurance to protect the homeowner and the lender against physical damage to a property from sources such as but not limited to fire, wind, or vandalism.

Insured Deposits: Deposits held in financial institutions that are guaranteed by the Federal Deposit Insurance Corporation (FDIC) against loss due to bank failure.

Interest: The term interest is used to describe the cost of using money, a right, share, or title in property.

Interest Rate: The amount paid by a borrower to a lender in exchange for the use of the lender's money for a certain period of time. Interest is paid on loans or on debt instruments, such as notes or bonds, either at regular intervals or as part of a lump sum payment when the issue matures.

Interest Rate Index: IA table of yields or interest rates being paid on debt that is used to determine interest-rate changes for adjustable-rate mortgages and other variable-rate loans.

J

Joint Account: An account owned by two or more persons. Either party can conduct transactions separately or together as set forth in the deposit account contract.

K

Kiting: Writing a cheque in an amount that will overdraw the account but making up the deficiency by depositing another cheque on another bank. For example, mailing a cheque for the mortgage when your cheque account has insufficient funds to cover the cheque, but counting on receiving and depositing your pay-cheque before the mortgage company presents the cheque for payment.

L

Late Charge: The fee charged for delinquent payment on an instalment loan, usually expressed as a percentage of the loan balance or payment. Also, a penalty imposed by a card issuer against a cardholder's account for failing to make minimum payments.

Lease: A contract transferring the use of property or occupancy of land, space, structures, or equipment in consideration of a payment (e.g. rent).

Lender: An individual or financial institution that lends money with the expectation that the money will be returned with interest.

Lien: Legal claim against a property. Once the property is sold, the lien holder is then paid the amount that is owed.

Line of Credit: A pre-approved loan authorization with a specific borrowing limit based on creditworthiness. A line of credit allows borrowers to obtain a number of loans without re-applying each time as long as the total of borrowed funds does not exceed the credit limit.

Loan-to-Value Ratio (LTV): The ratio of the loan principal (amount borrowed) to the appraised value (selling price). For example, on a US$ 100,000 home, with a mortgage loan principal of US$ 80,000, the loan-to-value ratio is 80 percent. The LTV will affect programs available to the borrower; generally, the lower the LTV, the more favourable the program terms offered by lenders.

Loan Contract: The written agreement between a borrower and a lender in which the terms and conditions of the loan are set.

Loan Fee: A fee charged by a lender to make a loan (in addition to the interest charged to the borrower).

Loan Modification Provision: A contractual agreement in a loan that allows the borrower or lender to permanently change one or more of the terms of the original contract.

Loan Proceeds: The net amount of funds that a lending institution disburses under the terms of a loan, and which the borrower then owes.

Local Cheque: A cheque payable by, at, or through a bank in the same cheque processing region as the location of the branch of the depository bank. The depository bank is the bank into which the cheque was deposited. As of February 27, 2010, the Federal Reserve consolidated its cheque processing centres into one processing centre. Therefore, all cheques are now considered local.

M

Manufactured (mobile) home: A structure, built on a

permanent chassis, transported to a site in one or more sections, and affixed to a permanent foundation. The term does not include recreational vehicles.

Maturity: The date on which the principal balance of a loan, bond, or other financial instrument becomes due and payable.

Media: Any organization in the business of informing the public with news or commentary. The various forms of media include print, television, internet, and radio.

Minimum Balance: The amount of money required to be on deposit in an account to qualify the depositor for special services or to waive a service charge.

Minimum Payment: The minimum dollar amount that must be paid each month on a loan, line of credit, or other debt.

Missing Payment: A payment that has been made but not credited to the appropriate account.

Mobile Home: To be eligible for coverage under the National Flood Insurance Program, a mobile home must be on a permanent foundation and meet specific anchoring requirements for it location.

Money Market Deposit Account: A savings account that offers a higher rate of interest in exchange for larger than normal deposits. Insured by the FDIC, these accounts have limits on the number of transactions allowed and may require higher balances to receive the higher rate of interest.

Mortgage: A debt instrument used in a real estate transaction where the property is the collateral for the loan. A mortgage gives the lender a right to take possession of the property if the borrower fails to pay off the loan.

Mortgage Loan: A loan made by a lender to a borrower for the financing of real property.

Mortgagee: The lender in a mortgage loan relationship.

Mortgagor: The borrower in a mortgage loan relationship

(Property is used as collateral to make payment).

Mutual Fund: A fund operated by an investment company that raises money from shareholders and invests it in stocks, bonds, options, commodities, or money market securities. These funds offer investors the advantages of diversification and professional management. To participate, the investor may pay fees and expenses.

N

National Credit Union Administration (NCUA): The Federal regulatory agency that charters and supervises Federal credit unions (NCUA also administers the National Credit Union Share Insurance Fund, which insures the deposits of Federal credit unions).

Not Automatically Protected: There are several types of Federal benefits that are not automatically protected under 31CFR 212: Federal benefits received by cheque rather than direct deposit; Federal benefits received more than two months before the bank received the garnishment order or Federal benefits that were transferred to another bank account. The benefits may be exempt from garnishment but you will have to alert the court or creditor.

O

Official Cheque: A cheque drawn on a bank and signed by an authorized bank official (Also known as a cashier's cheque).

Offset, Right of: Banks' legal right to seize funds that a guarantor or debtor may have on deposit to cover a loan in default. It is also known as right of setoff

Online Banking: A service that allows an account holder to obtain account information and manage certain banking transactions through a personal computer via the financial institution's web site on the Internet (This is also known as Internet or electronic banking).

Open-End Credit: A credit agreement (typically a credit card)

that allows a customer to borrow against a pre-approved credit line when purchasing goods and services. The borrower is only billed for the amount that is actually borrowed plus any interest due (Also called a charge account or revolving credit).

Operating Subsidiary: National banks conduct some of their banking activities through companies called operating subsidiaries. These subsidiaries are companies that are owned or controlled by a national bank and that, among other things, offer banking products and services such as loans, mortgages, and leases. The Office of the Comptroller of the Currency supervises and regulates the activities of many of these operating subsidiaries.

Outstanding Cheque: A cheque written by a depositor that has not yet been presented for payment to or paid by the depositor's bank.

Overdraft: When the amount of money withdrawn from a bank account is greater than the amount actually available in the account, the excess is known as an overdraft, and the account is said to be overdrawn.

Overdraw: To write a cheque for an amount that exceeds the amount on deposit in the account.

Over Limit: An open-end credit account in which the assigned dollar limit has been exceeded.

P

Participating Community: A community for which the Federal Emergency Management Agency (FEMA) has authorized the sale of flood insurance under the National Flood Insurance Program (NFIP).

Passbook: A book in ledger form in which are recorded all deposits, withdrawals, and earnings of a customer's savings account.

Past Due Item: Any note or other time instrument of indebtedness that has not been paid on the due date.

Payday Loans: A small-dollar, short-term loan that a borrower promises to repay out of their next pay-cheque or deposit of funds.

Payee: The person or organization to whom a cheque, draft, or note is made payable.

Paying Bank: A bank upon which a cheque is drawn and that pays a cheque or other draft.

Payment Due Date: The date on which a loan or instalment payment is due. It is set by a financial institution. Any payment received after this date is considered late; fees and penalties can be assessed.

Payoff: The complete repayment of a loan, including principal, interest, and any other amounts due. Payoff occurs either over the full term of the loan or through prepayments.

Payoff Statement: A formal statement prepared when a loan payoff is contemplated. It shows the current status of the loan account, all sums due, and the daily rate of interest.

Payer: The person or organization who pays.

Periodic Rate: The interest rate described in relation to a specific amount of time. The monthly periodic rate, for example, is the cost of credit per month; the daily periodic rate is the cost of credit per day.

Periodic Statement: The billing summary produced and mailed at specified intervals, usually monthly.

Personal Identification Number (PIN): Generally, a four-character number or word, the PIN is the secret code given to credit or debit cardholders enabling them to access their accounts. The code is either randomly assigned by the bank or selected by the customer. It is intended to prevent unauthorized use of the card while accessing a financial service terminal.

PITI: Common acronym for principal, interest, taxes, and insurance—used when describing the monthly charges on a mortgage.

Point of Sale (POS): (a) The location at which a transaction takes place, (b) Systems that allow bank customers to effect transfers of funds from their deposit accounts and other financial transactions at retail establishments.

Power of Attorney: A written instrument which authorizes one person to act as another's agent or attorney. The power of attorney may be for a definite, specific act, or it may be general in nature. The terms of the written power of attorney may specify when it will expire. If not, the power of attorney usually expires when the person granting it dies.

Some institutions require that you use the bank's power of attorney forms (The bank may refer to this as a Durable Power of Attorney: The principal grants specific rights to the agent).

Preauthorized Electronic Fund Transfers: An EFT authorized in advance to recur at substantially regular intervals.

Preauthorized Payment: A system established by a written agreement under which a financial institution is authorized by the customer to debit the customer's account in order to pay bills or make loan payments.

Preferred Risk Policy (PRP): A policy that offers fixed combinations of building/contents coverage or contents-only coverage at modest, fixed premiums. The PRP generally is available for property located in B, C, and X zones in Regular Program Communities that meets eligibility requirements based on the property's flood loss history.

Prepayment: The payment of a debt before it actually becomes due.

Prepayment Clause: A clause in a mortgage allowing the mortgagor to pay off part or all of the unpaid debt before it becomes due.

Prepayment Penalty: A penalty imposed on a borrower for repaying the loan before its due date (In the case of a mortgage, this applies when there is not a prepayment clause in the mortgage note to offset the penalty).

Previous Balance: The cardholder's account balance as of the previous billing statement.

Principal Balance: The outstanding balance on a loan, excluding interest and fees.

Private Mortgage Insurance (PMI): Insurance offered by a private insurance company that protects the bank against loss on a defaulted mortgage up to the limit of the policy (usually 20 to 25 percent of the loan amount). PMI is usually limited to loans with a high loan-to-value (LTV) ratio. The borrower pays the premium.

R

Reconciliation: The process of analyzing two related records and, if differences exist between them, finding the cause and bringing the two records into agreement. Example: Comparing an up-to-date cheque book with a monthly statement from the financial institution holding the account.

Redlining: The alleged practice of certain lending institutions of not making mortgage, home improvement, and small business loans in certain neighbourhoods-usually areas that are deteriorating or considered by the lender to be poor investments.

Refinancing: A way of obtaining a better interest rate, lower monthly payments, or borrow cash on the equity in a property that has built up on a loan. A second loan is taken out to pay off the first, higher-rate loan.

Refund: An amount paid back because of an overpayment or because of the return of an item previously sold.

Release of Lien: To free a piece of real estate from a mortgage.

Renewal: A form of extending an unpaid loan in which the borrower's remaining unpaid loan balance is carried over (renewed) into a new loan at the beginning of the next financing period.

Residual Interest: Interest that continues to accrue on your credit card balance from the statement cycle date until the bank receives your payment. For example, if your statement cycle date was January 10 and the bank received your payment on January 20, there were ten days for which interest accrued. This amount will be posted on your next statement.

Return Item: A negotiable instrument—principally a cheque—that has been sent to one bank for collection and payment and is returned unpaid by the sending bank.

Reverse Mortgage: A reverse mortgage is a special home loan product that allows a homeowner aged 62 or older the ability to access the equity that has accumulated in their home. The home itself will be the source of repayment. The loan is underwritten based on the value of the collateral (home) and the life expectancy of the borrower. The loan must be repaid when you die, sell your home, or no longer live there as your principal residence.

Revolving Credit: A credit agreement (typically a credit card) that allows a customer to borrow against a pre-approved credit line when purchasing goods and services. The borrower is only billed for the amount that is actually borrowed plus any interest due (Also called a charge account or open-end credit).

Right of Offset: Banks' legal right to seize funds that a guarantor or debtor may have on deposit to cover a loan in default. It is also known as the right of set-off.

Right of Rescission: Right to cancel, within three business days, a contract that uses the home of a person as collateral, except in the case of a first mortgage loan. There is no fee to the borrower, who receives a full refund of all fees paid. The right of rescission is guaranteed by the Truth in Lending Act (TILA).

S

Safe (or Safety) Deposit Box: A type of safe usually located in groups inside a bank vault and rented to customers for their use in storing valuable items.

Safekeeping: A service provided by banks where securities and valuables are protected in the vaults of the bank for customers.

Satisfaction of Mortgage: A document issued by a mortgagee (the lender) when a mortgage is paid in full.

Service Charge: A charge assessed by a depository institution for processing transactions and maintaining accounts.

Signature Card: A card signed by each depositor and customer of a bank which may be used as a means of identification. The signature card represents a contract between the bank and the depositor.

Stale-Dated Cheque: Presented to the paying bank 180 days (6 months) or more after the original issue date. Banks are not required by the Uniform Commercial Code to honour stale-dated cheques and can return them to the issuing bank unpaid. The maker of a cheque can discourage late presentment by writing the words "not good after X days" on the back of the cheque.

Statement: A summary of all transactions that occurred over the preceding month and could be associated with a deposit account or a credit card account.

Stop Payment: An order not to pay a cheque that has been issued but not yet cashed. If requested soon enough, the cheque will not be debited from the payer's account. Most banks charge a fee for this service.

Student Loan: Loans made, insured, or guaranteed under any program authorized by the Higher Education Act. Loan funds are used by the borrower for education purposes.

T

Terms: The period of time and the interest rate arranged between creditor and debtor to repay a loan.

Time Certificate of Deposit: A time deposit evidenced by a negotiable or nonnegotiable instrument specifying an amount and maturity.

Time Deposit: A time deposit (also known as a term deposit) is a money deposit at a bank that cannot be withdrawn for a certain "term" or period of time. When the term is over it can be withdrawn, or it can be held for another term. The longer the term, the better the yield on the money. Generally, there are significant penalties for early withdrawal.

Trust Account: A general term that covers all types of accounts in a trust department, such as estates, guardianships, and agencies.

Trust Administrator: A person or institution that manages trust accounts.

U

Uncollected Funds: A portion of a deposit balance that has not yet been collected by the depository bank.

Uniform Commercial Code (UCC): A set of statutes enacted by the various States to provide consistency among the States' commercial laws. It includes negotiable instruments, sales, stock transfers, trust and warehouse receipts, and bills of lading.

Usury: Charging an illegally high interest rate on a loan.

Usury Rates: The maximum rate of interest lenders may charge borrowers. The usury rate is generally set by State law.

V

Variable Rate: Any interest rate or dividend that changes on a periodic basis.

Bibliography/References

Bibliography/References

Achanta, R.N.S.P. (1998), The Banking (Regulation) Act,1949 Along With Banking Regulation (Companies) Rules, Reserve Bank of India Act and Allied Laws, India Capital Bureau, Bangalore.

Ahmed, Fakhruddin Ali (1972), Co-operatives: Social Justice and Common Service, *Indian Co-operative Review*, NCUI, New Delhi, April.

Ambruster, P. (2001), Co-operative Banks in Europe: Values and Practices to Promote Development, *IRU Courier* (3).

Basak, Amit (2010), Co-operative Banks in India, New Century Publications, New Delhi, India.

Bedi, Raghubans Dev (1969), Theory, History and Practice of Co-operation, Loyal Book Depot, Meerut.

Biety, Monnie, (2003), "Liquidity and Asset Liability Management," in Savings Services for the Poor: An Operational Guide (ed.) Madeline Hirschland, Washington, D.C.: PACT Publications.

Biety, Monnie (1998), Operational Guidelines for the Development and Early Stages of Credit Union Operations, Madison, Wis.: World Council of Credit Unions, Inc.

Biety, Monnie, Madeline Hirschland, and Kathleen Stack (1999), Credit with Education and Credit Unions Strategic Planning Guidelines, Pact Publications, Washington, D.C.

Chakraborty, B. (1998), Resource Management: An Appraisal of the Nadia District Central Co-operative Bank, *Co-operative Perspective*, Vaikunthlal Mehata National Institute of Cooperative Management, Pune, January-March.

Chavez, Jesus R. (2002), Management Assessment Guide for Credit Unions.

Chinchankar, P.Y. and Namjoshi, M.V. (1977), Co-operation and the Dynamics of Change, Somaiya Publications Pvt. Ltd., New Delhi.

Choubey, B.N. (1986), Cooperative Banking in India, Asia Publishing, Bombay, India.

Cuevas C.E. and Fisher K.P. (2006), Cooperative Financial Institutions: Issues in Governance, Regulation and Supervision, World Bank, Working Paper No. 82.

Dantwala, M.L. and Barmeda, J.N. (1986), "Rural Development, Approaches and Issues" in Dantwala, M.L. and others (ed.) Indian Agricultural Development since Independence, Indian Society of Agricultural Economics.

David, C. Richardson (2002), Pearls Monitoring System, World Council of Credit Unions, October.

David, C. Richardson (2000), "Model Credit Unions in the Twenty First Century", in Safe Money (eds.) G. Westley and B. Branch, IDB.

Dharia, Mohan (1984), Co-operative Movement: Essentials, *Indian Co-operative Review*, NCUI, January.

Dubhashi, P.R. (1988), *Principles and Philosophy of Co-operation*, Vaikunth Mehata National Institute of Co-operative Management, Pune.

Dutta, Uttam and Basak, Amit (2008), "Appraisal of Financial Performance of Urban Co-operative Banks: A Case Study", *The Management Accountant*, March.

Dutta, S.K. (1991), Co-operative Societies and Rural Development, Mittal Publications, New Delhi.

Dwivedi, R.C. (1981), Co-operative Movement versus Politics: Profile of Indian Situation, *Indian Cooperative Review*, NCUI, New Delhi, January.

Elayath, K.M.N. (1984), New Vistas on Co-operative Management, Rainbow Publications, Coimbatore.

Ghosh, Pratyush Prasun (1992), Public Administration and Co-operative Management: A New Dimension, W. Newman and Company Ltd., Calcutta.

Goel, G.B and Powan, K. Kamra (1988), Co-operatives Hold the Key to Rural Development, *Kurukshetra,* February.

Gulati, Ashok (1998), *Indian Agriculture in an Open Economy: Will it Prosper?* in Isher Judge Ahluwalia and I.M.D. Little (eds.), India's Economic Reforms and Development: Essays for Manmohan Singh, Oxford University Press, New Delhi.

Gulati, Ashok (1996), *Reforms and Policies for Agriculture*, in Vijay L. Kelkar and V.V. Bhanoji Rao (eds.), Development Policy Imperatives, Tata McGraw-Hill, New Delhi.

Hesse, H. and Cihàk, M. (2007), Cooperative Banks and Financial Stability, IMF Working Paper.

Hough, E.M. (1966), Co-operative Movement in India, Oxford University Press, New Delhi.

Indian Institute of Banking and Finance (2007), Laws of Cooperative Banking, Macmillan Publishers, India.

Iyengar, A.S.K. (1961), A Study in the Co-operative Movement in India, Current Book House, Bombay.

Jain, Pramod Lata (1990), Co-operative Credit in Rural India, Mittal Publications, New Delhi.

Kamat, G.S. (1978), New Dimensions of Co-operative Management, Himalaya Publishing House, Bombay.

Kamat, G.S. (1986), Co-operatives and Poverty Removal, *Kurukshetra,* November-December.

Karve, D.G. (1969), *Co-operation: Principles and Substance*, Gokhale Institute of Politics and Economics, Asia Publishing House, Bombay.

Klaehn, Janette, Anna Cora Evans and Brian Branch (2002), A Technical Guide to Savings Mobilization: Lessons from the Credit Union Experience, World Council of Credit Unions Inc., Madison, Wisconsin.

Krishna, D. (1998), Peace, Progress and Prosperity through Urban Co-operative Banks, *The Co-operator*, Vol. 36, No. 5, NCUI, New Delhi.

Krishna, D. (2002), Future Strategies to Strengthen the Urban Co-operative Banks, *The Co-operator*, Vol. 40, No. 5, NCUI, New Delhi.

Krishnaswami, O.R. (1968), An Overview of Principles of Co-operation, *Indian Co-operative Review,* No. 1, NCUI, New Delhi.

Krishnaswami, O.R. (1978), Fundamentals of Co-operation, S. Chand and Company Ltd., New Delhi.

Kulandaiswamy, V. (1974), Creation of Common Cadres in Co-operatives, *Indian Co-operative Review,* NCUI, New Delhi, April.

Kulkarni, K.R. (1955), Theory and Practice of Co-operation in India and Abroad, The Co-operator's Book Depot, Bombay.

Laud, G.M. (1980), Co-operative Banking in India, Sage Publications, New Delhi.

Mamoria, C.B. and Saxena, R.D. (1970), Co-operation in India, Oxford University Press, New Delhi.

Mohanan, S. and Benson Kunjukunju (2002), Credit Through Co-operatives: Problems and Solutions, *The Co-operator*, Vol. 40, No. 1, NCUI, New Delhi.

Nakkiran, S. (1980), Cooperative Banking in India, Rainbow Publications, Coimbatore.

Nanda, K.C. (1989), Credit and Banking, Sage Publications India Pvt. Ltd., New Delhi.

Nayak, Umesh Chandra and Roy, Ananta Kumar (1988), Co-operation and Co-operative Management, Kalyani Publishers, New Delhi.

Patnaik, Surendra (1999), Co-operative Banking in India, *The Co-operator*, Vol. 37, No. 5, NCUI, New Delhi.

Pitre, V. (2003), Urban Co-operative Banks: Issues and Prospects, *Economic and Political Weekly*, Vol. XXXVIII, No. 15, April 12.

Prabhu, P.V. (1999), Urban Co-operative Banking in India, *Urban Credit*, Vol. 14, No. 3, NAFCUB, New Delhi.

Puri, S.S. (1973), Co-operatives: An Assessment of Work and Growth, *Indian Co-operative Review,* NCUI, New Delhi, April.

Puri, S.S. (1985), Ends and Means of Co-operative Development, National Co-operative Union of India, New Delhi.

Quaraishi, M.A. (1974), Democracy and Efficiency in Thrift and Credit Co-operatives, *Indian Co-operative Review,* NCUI, New Delhi, July.

Raikar, A.V. (2003), Growth, Profitability and Cost Efficiency of Urban Co-operative Banks in India: A Comparative Analysis, *Indian Co-operative Review*, Vol. 42, No. 2, NCUI, New Delhi.

Ramesh, T. (2007), Structural Reforms in Co-operative Banking, *The Management Accountant*, ICWAI, Vol. 42, No. 2, February.

Rana, J.M. (1972), *Education and Leadership for Co-operative Democracy in India*, International Co-operative Alliance, New Delhi.

Rao, Hanumantha C.H. (1995), Liberalization of Agriculture in India-Some Major Issues, *Indian Journal of Agricultural Economics*, No. 3.

Rao, Hanumantha C.H. (1999), *Changing Economic Structure of the Rural Economy in Asia and the Pacific,* paper presented at the study meeting on Rural Transformation, held at Yogakarta, Indonesia, November 29 to December 3.

Rao, K. Viswanadha and V. Mohandoss (1986), Co-operative Credit: Certain Dimensions and Problems, *Indian Co-operative Review,* NCUI, New Delhi, January.

Raviprasad, S. (2004), Performance of Urban Co-operative Banks:

Some Aspects, *The Co-operator,* Vol. 41, No. 10, NCUI, New Delhi.

Rayudu, C.S. (1991), Rural Credit in India, Mittal Publications, New Delhi.

Richard, John Pelrine (2001), Rural finance Adviser for ACDI-VOCA/Ethiopia, Selected readings for the promotion and management of SACCOs, December.

Richardson, David C. (2001), Pearls Monitoring System, WOCCU Toolkit Series: Number 4, World Council of Credit Unions Inc., Madison, Wisconsin.

Sangwan, S.S. (1998), Emerging Issues of Indian Peasantry, *Yojana*, October, Vol. 42, No. 10.

Saxena, K.K. (1973), Evolution of Co-operative Thoughts, Orient Longman, New Delhi.

Sharma, Prem S. (1999), Co-operative Banking at Crossroads, *The Co-operator*, Vol. 37, No. 6, NCUI, New Delhi.

Sheshadri, P. (1973), Latest Developments in Co-operative Legislation, *Indian Co-operative Review,* NCUI, New Delhi, April.

Singh, Katar (2002), Co-operation as an Instrument of Rural Development, *Kurukshetra*, February.

Sinha, B.K. (1968), *Co-operatives in India*, National Co-operative Union of India, New Delhi.

Siosodia, S.S. (1997), Urban Co-operative Sector: Its Importance and Needs Assessment, *The Co-operator*, Vol. 33, No. 5, NCUI, New Delhi.

Sisodia, S.S. (1997), Urban Co-operative Credit and Sustainable Human Development in India, *The Co-operator*, Vol. 34, No. 7, NCUI, New Delhi.

Soni, Monica (2002), NPA Management by Rural Banks: A Critical Appraisal, *Indian Journal of Accounting*, IAA, Vol. XXXIII, December.

Sreenivasulu, D. (2003), Urban Co-operative Banks: Maclagan to Madhav Rao, *The Co-operator*, Vol. 40, No. 11, NCUI, New Delhi.

Srinath, A.R. (2000), Co-operative Credit in India: Problems and Suggestions, *The Co-operator*, Vol. 38, No. 1, NCUI, New Delhi.

Srivastava, G.P. (1962), *Traditional Forms of Co-operation in India*, Indian Co-operative Union, New Delhi.

Stephenson, T.E. (1963), Management in Co-operative Societies, Heinemann Ltd., London.

Taimni, K.K. (1976), *Co-operative Organisation and Management*, W.A.F.M. Farmers Welfare Trust Society, New Delhi.

Thakur, D.S. (1973), Small Farmers and Co-operative Overdues: Views, *Indian Co-operative Review,* NCUI, New Delhi, April.

Thamarajakshi, R. (1999), Agriculture and Economic Reforms, *Economic and Political Weekly*, Vol. 34, No. 33.

Thirunarayanan, R. (1996), Co-operative Banking in India, Mittal Publications, New Delhi.

Thirunarayanan, R. (1998), Urban Bank to the Rescue of the Needy, *The Co-operator*, Vol. 35, No. 12, NCUI, New Delhi.

Tribhuvan, Mahal (1996), Long-term Co-operative Financing System under New Economic Policy, *Land Bank Journal*, Vol. 35, No. 1.

Tules, Robby (1995), Poverty Alleviation and Role of Credit Co-operatives, *The Co-operator*, Vol. 32, No. 9, NCUI, New Delhi.

Tyagi, Lalit Kumar and Rashmi Singh (1998), Rural Credit Delivery System: Neglected Dimensions and Needed Focus, *Kurukshetra,* Vol. 46, No. 9.

Tyagi, R.B. (1968), Recent Trends in the Co-operative Movement in India, Asia Publishing House, Bombay.

Upadhya, Vidya V. and Vasan, B. Kodag (1996), Women's Role in Urban Co-operative Banks with Special Reference to Sri Laxmi Mahila Sahakari Bank Limited, Sangli, *Indian Co-operative Review,* Vol. 34, No. 7, NCUI.

Viswanathan (1997), Future Role and Place of Co-operative Credit and Banking Sector in Asia with Particular Reference to Indian Situations, *The Co-operator,* Vol. 34, No. 7, NCUI.

Vyas, V.S. (2001), Agriculture: Second Round of Economic Reforms, *Economic and Political Weekly*, Vol. 36, No. 10.

Weeraman, P.E. (1973), The Co-operative Principles, *Indian Co-operative Review,* April, NCUI.

Index

Index